HARRAP'S

Chinese

PHRASE BOOK

Compiled by
LEXUS
with
Yu Mei Zhang
and
Tom Mitford

GW00319762

HARRAP

London Paris

First published in Great Britain 1990
by HARRAP BOOKS LTD
Chelsea House, 26 Market Square,
Bromley, Kent BR1 1NA

© *Harrap Books Ltd/Lexus Ltd* 1990

ISBN 0 245-54937-4

Reprinted 1990

Printed and bound in Singapore by
Intellectual Publishing Co.

CONTENTS

PINYIN

Pinyin is a commonly used method for writing Chinese in the roman alphabet. But since it is not a pronunciation system in the sense in which phrase books traditionally understand pronunciation systems, we have not used Pinyin in this book.

If you do come across Chinese written in Pinyin the following 'code table' will help you decipher how the Pinyin is pronounced.

consonants

c	like 'ts' in 'hats'
q	like 'ch' in 'chin'
x	like the 's-y' sound in 'this year'
z	like 'ds' in 'fads'
zh	like 'j' in 'James'

vowels and vowel combinations

a	as in 'rather'
ai	as in 'Shanghai'
ei	as in 'Beijing' or 'weight'
i	pronounced as in 'Maria' except in the following combinations: $ci, chi, ri, si, shi, zi, zhi$ In these combinations the 'i' is pronounced as in 'sir' (see also page 6)
ia	as in 'yarn'
ian	as in 'yen'
iang	pronounced 'yarng'
ie	as in 'yet'
iu	as in 'yodel'
o	as in 'for'
ou	as in 'dough'
u	as in 'Zulu' (but in some cases as below for ü)
ui	is pronounced 'way'
uo	is pronounced 'war'
ü	as in 'few' (it's the French sound as in 'du')

4

INTRODUCTION

The phrase sections in this book are concise and to the point. In each section you will find: a list of basic vocabulary; a selection of useful phrases; a list of common words and expressions that you will see on signs and notices. A full pronunciation guide is given for things you'll want to say or ask and typical replies to some of your questions are listed.

Of course, there are bound to be occasions when you want to know more. So this book allows for this by giving an English-Chinese dictionary with a total of some 1,600 references. This will enable you to build up your Chinese vocabulary and to make variations on the phrases in the phrase sections.

As well as this we have given a menu reader covering about 200 dishes and types of food — so that you will know what you are ordering! And, as a special feature, there is a section on colloquial Chinese.

The section on China and Things Chinese gives cultural information about China as well as some notes on the language.

This book uses Standard Chinese and simplified characters.

Speaking the language can make all the difference to your trip. So:

祝好运！

jù hǎo yèwn!
good luck!

and

一路顺风！

éelù shùnfērng!
have a good trip!

5

In the phrase sections of this book a pronunciation
guide has been given by writing the Chinese words as
though they were English. If you read out the
pronunciation as English words (and pay attention to
the tones) a Chinese should be able to understand you.
Some notes on the pronunciation system:

ao	as in 'Mao'
ay	as in 'day'
e, eh	as in 'bed'
ee	as in 'feet'
er	as in 'her'
ew	as in 'dew' (if you know French, it's the 'u' sound)
I	as the 'i' sound in 'high'
j	as in 'jockey'
ir	for example in 'shir': if you say 'shred' slowly (sh-red) then 'shr' is the 'shir' sound
u	as in 'Zulu'
y	is always as in 'you' and never as in 'why'

TONES

What is difficult, and essential, are the tones. Words
are pitched — almost sung — and if a tone is wrong, the
meaning could be lost. These tones are familiar in
English, but whereas in English they express surprise
or hesitation or sharpness etc (oh?, no!, so what!, hey
ho!), in Chinese they determine meaning.

There are four tones in Mandarin Chinese: high level
(1st) ˉ, rising (2nd) ´, low (3rd) ˇ and falling (4th) `:

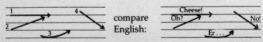

Some tones disappear in rapid speech.

GENERAL PHRASES

hello, hi
née hǎo!

你好！

good morning
dzǎosharng hǎo!

早上好！

good evening
wǎnsharng hǎo!

晚上好！

good night
wǎn ān!

晚安！

pleased to meet you
jyèndào nĕe hĕn
gāosyìng

见到你很高兴

goodbye
dzĭ jyèn!

再见！

cheerio
hwáytó jyèn

回头见

yes (*see grammar*)
shìrder

是的

no (*see grammar*)
bù

不

yes please
hǎoder

好的

no thank you
bú yòngler, syèh·syeh

不用了，谢谢

please
chĭng

请

please do
bú kèrchee

不客气

GENERAL PHRASES

thank you/thanks
syèh·syeh
谢谢

thank you very much
fāychárng gǎnsyèh
非常感谢

you're welcome
bú kèrchee
不客气

sorry
dwàybuchěe
对不起

sorry? (*didn't understand*)
shémmer?
什么？

how are you?
née hǎo ma?
你好吗？

very well, thank you
hén hǎo, syèh·syeh
很好，谢谢

and yourself?
něe ner?
你呢？

excuse me (*to get attention*)
láo jyà!
劳驾！

how much is it?
dwōrshao chyén?
多少钱？

can I ...?
wǒr kér·ee ... ma?
我可以……吗？

can I have ...?
wǒr kér·ee ... ma?
我可以……吗？

I'd like to ...
wór syǎrng ...
我想……

where is ...?
... dzǐ nǎlee?
……在哪里？

it's not ...
bú shìr ...
不是……

GENERAL PHRASES

is it ...?
shìr ... ma?

是……吗？

is there ... here?
jèrr yŏ ... ma?

这儿有……吗？

could you say that again?
něe nérng dzł shwŏr
ēebyèn ma?

你能再说一遍吗？

please don't speak so fast
chĭng bú yào jyărng
jèrmer kwŘ

请不要讲这么快

I don't understand
wŏr bù míngbí

我不明白

OK
hăo ba

好吧

come on, let's go!
kwŘ dyĕn, wŏrmen dzŏ
ba!

快点，我们走吧！

what's your name?
něe jyào shemmer
míngdzìr?

你叫什么名字？

(more polite)
něe gwày·syìng?

你贵姓？

what's that in Chinese?
jèr dzł Jŏngwénlee jyào
shemmer?

这在中文里叫什么？

**could you write that down
please?**
chíng syĕh éesyà

请写一下

that's fine!
hăo ba!

好吧！

I don't speak Chinese
wŏr búhwày jyărng
Hànyĕw

我不会讲汉语

GENERAL PHRASES

请勿乱踏草地	chǐngwù lwàntà tsǎodèe **keep off the grass**	女厕(所)	něw tsèr(swǒr) **ladies**
请勿随地乱扔纸屑	chǐngwù swáydèe lwànrērng jǐr·syewěh **no litter**	入口	rùkǒ **way in**
请勿随地吐痰	chǐngwù swáydèe tútán **no spitting**	推	twāy **push**
出口	chūkǒ **way out**	危险	wǎysyēn **danger**
公共厕所	gōnggòng tsèrswǒr **public toilets**	外国人未经许可, 禁止超越	wīgwórrén wày jīng syéwkěr, jìnjǐr chāo·yewěh **no foreigners beyond this point without permission**
公厕	gōngtsèr **public toilets**	油漆未干	yóchēe wàygān **wet paint**
军事要地, 请勿靠近	jēwnshìr yàodèe, chǐngwù kàojìn **military zone, keep out**		
禁止……	jìnjǐr … **… forbidden**		
禁止拍照	jìnjǐr pǐjào **no photographs**		
禁止停车	jìnjǐr tíngchěr **no parking**		
拉	lā **pull**		
男厕(所)	nán tsèr(swǒr) **gents**		

COMING AND GOING

airport fāyjēechárng	飞机场	**harbour** gárngkǒ	港口
baggage syínglee	行李	**plane** fāyjēe	飞机
book (*in advance*) yèwdìng	预订	**sleeper** wòrpù	卧铺
coach chárngtú chēechēr	长途汽车	**station** chērjàn	车站
bus gōnggòng chēechēr	公共汽车	**taxi** chūdzū chèechēr	出租汽车
docks mǎtó	码头	**ticket** pyào	票
ferry dùchwán	渡船	**train** hwǒrchēr	火车
gate (*at airport*) dērng·jēekǒ	登机口		

a ticket to ...
dào ... der pyào

到……的票

I'd like to reserve a seat
wór syǎrng yèwdìng éegèr
dzòrwày

我想预订一个座位

smoking/non-smoking please
syēeyēnchēw/fāy
syēeyēnchēw

吸烟区 / 非吸烟区

a window seat please
chīng dìng éegèr
kàochwǎrng der
dzwòrwày

请订一个靠窗的座位

11

COMING AND GOING

which platform is it for ...?
dào ... dzž dèe jěe jàntí?

到……在第几站台？

what time is the next flight?
syà ēe hárngbān
jéedyěnjōng?

下一航班几点钟？

is this the right train for ...?
jèr shìr dào ... der
hwǒrchēr ma?

这是到……的火
车吗？

is this bus going to ...?
jèr lyàrng chēr dào ...
ma?

这辆车到……吗？

is this seat free?
jèr wàydzir yǒ rén dzwòr
ma?

这位子有人坐吗？

**do I have to change
(trains)?**
wǒr syēw·yào hwàn
chēr ma?

我需要换车吗？

is this the right stop for ...?
dào ... dzž jèrlee syàchēr
ma?

到……在这里下车吗？

is this ticket ok?
jèr jārng pyào yǒsyào
ma?

这张票有效吗？

I want to change my ticket
wór syǎrng hwàn jārng
pyào

我想换张票

thanks for a lovely stay
syèh·syèh něeder jāodì

谢谢你的招待

(said to a group)
syèh·syèh něemender
jāodì

谢谢你们的招待

12

COMING AND GOI

**thanks very much for
coming to meet me**
fäychárng gǎnsyèh nĕe
lí jyēh wǒr

非常感谢你来接我

well, here we are in . . .
syèndzǐ wǒrmen dàoler . . .

现在我们到了……

有东西要申报吗？

yǒ dōngsyee yào
shēnbào ma?
anything to declare?

请打开这个包，行吗？

chíng dǎkī jèrger bāo,
syíng ma?
would you mind opening
this bag please?

办理登机手 续，托运 行李	bànlěe dēngjēe shǒsyèw, twōryèwn syínglěe **check-in**	电话亭	dyènhwàtíng **public telephone**
长途汽车站	chárngtú chèechēr jàn **coach station**	非吸烟区	fāy syēeyēnchēw **no smoking**
起飞时间	chěefāy shírjyěn **departure time(s)**	公用电话	gōngyòng dyènhwà **public telephone**
请勿吸烟	chíngwù syēeyēn **no smoking**	国际航班	gwórjèe hárngbān **international departures**
出租汽车	chūdzūchèechēr **taxi**	国内航班	gwórnày hárngbān **domestic departures**
登机口	dēngjēekǒ **gate**	候车室	hòchērshìr **waiting room**

13

COMING AND GOING

候机室   hòujēeshìr
**departure
lounge**

火车站   hwŏrchērjàn
station

站台票   jàntípyào
platform tickets

系好安全带   jèehǎo
ānchwéndì
fasten seatbelts

中国国际旅   Jōnggwór
行社   gwórjèe
lěwsyíngshèr
**China
International
Travel Service**

中国海关   Jōnggwór
hǐgwān
**Chinese
customs**

老人孕妇专座   lǎorén yèwnfù
jwāndzwòr
**reserved for the
elderly and
pregnant
women**

列车到站时   lyèchēr dàojàn
刻表   shírkèrbyǎo
**train arrival
time(s)**

免税商店   myěnshwày
shāngdyèn
duty-free shop

男厕(所)   nán tsèr(swŏr)
gents

女厕(所)   něw
tsèr(swŏr)
ladies

软席车   rwǎnsyéechēr
**soft seat
carriage (more
expensive)**

软卧车   rwǎnwòrchēr
**soft sleeper
carriage (luxury)**

售票口   shòupyàokŏ
ticket office

吸烟区   syēeyēnchēw
smoking

行李寄存   syínglěe
jèetsún
left luggage

行李领取   syínglěe
处   língchěwchù
baggage claim

太平门   tìpíngmén
emergency exit

厕所   tsèrswŏr
toilet

问讯处   wènsyèwnchù
enquiries

硬席车   yìngsyéechēr
**hard seat
carriage (cheapest
seats)**

硬卧车   yìngwòrchēr
**hard sleeper
carriage (cheaper
sleeper)**

balcony yárng·tí	阳台	**key** yàoshir	钥匙
bed chwárng	床	**lunch** wǔfàn	午饭
breakfast dzǎofàn	早饭	**night** yèh	夜
dinner wǎnfàn	晚饭	**private bathroom** sīrén syéedzǎojyēn	私人洗澡间
dining room tsāntīng	餐厅	**reception** jyēdìchù	接待处
double room shwārng·rén fárng·jyēn	双人房间	**room** fárng·jyēn	房间
hostel lěw·dyèn	旅店	**shower** línyèh	淋浴
hotel (small) léw·gwǎn	旅馆	**single room** dānrén fárng·jyēn	单人房间
(catering for Westerners) fàndyèn	饭店	**with bath** dì yèwshìr	带浴室

do you have a room?
yǒ fárng·jyēn ma?

有房间吗?

just for one night
jǐr jù ēeyèh

只住一夜

do you have a room for one person?
yǒ dānrén fárng·jyēn ma?

有单人房间吗?

15

GETTING A ROOM

do you have a room for two people?
yŏ shwārng·rén
fárng·jyēn ma?

有双人房间吗？

I'm looking for a good cheap room
wór syárng jăo éegèr
tyáojyèn bútswòr yò
pyénèe der fárng·jyēn

我想找一个条件不错
又便宜的房间

I have a reservation
wór éejīng yèwdìngler

我已经预订了

how much is it?
dwōrshao chyén?

多少钱？

can I see the room please?
wŏr nérng kànkàn
fárng·jyēn ma?

我能看看房间吗？

does that include breakfast?
jèrger jyáchyén bāokwòr
dzăofàn ma?

这个价钱包括早饭吗？

a room overlooking the sea
fŭkàn dàhī der
fárng·jyēn

俯瞰大海的房间

we'd like to stay another night
wŏrmen syărng dzĭ jù
éeyèh

我们想再住一夜

we will be arriving late (*late at night*)
wŏrmen jyārng
shēnyèh dàodá

我们将深夜到达

(*later than planned*)
wŏrmen jyārng
wănsyeh shírhò dàodá

我们将晚些时候到达

16

GETTING A ROOM

can I have my bill please?
wŏr kér·ee fùjàrng ma?

我可以付账吗？

I'll pay cash
wŏr yòng syènkwăn fù

我用现款付

can I pay by credit card?
wŏr kér·ee yòng syìnyòng
kă fùjàrng ma?

我可以用信用卡
付账吗？

**will you give me a call at
6.30 in the morning?**
née dzăoshàrng
lyòdyĕnbàn jyàosyíng
wŏr, syíngma?

你早上六点半叫醒我，
行吗？

**at what time do you serve
breakfast/dinner?**
dzăofàn/wănfàn jée
dyĕn?

早饭/晚饭几点？

**can we have breakfast in
our room?**
wŏrmen kér·ee dzĭ
dzìrjĕe fárng·jyĕnlĕe
yòng dzăofàn ma?

我们可以在自己房间
里用早饭吗？

thanks for putting us up
syèh·syèh dwày
wŏrmender jyĕdì

谢谢对我们的接待

请勿打搅	chĭngwù dájyăo **please do not disturb**	电梯	dyèntēe **lift**
		一楼	ēeló **first floor**
地下室	dèesyàshìr **basement**	二楼	èrló **second floor**

GETTING A ROOM

饭店	fàndyèn **hotel** (*Western-style hotel*)	餐厅	tsāntīng **dining room, restaurant**
服务台	fúwùtí **reception**	无人	wúrén **free**
工艺美术服 务部	gōng·èe mǎyshù fúwùbù **arts and crafts shop**	游艺室	yó·èeshìr **recreation room**
关	gwān **closed**	有人	yǒrén **engaged**
招待所	jāodìswǒr **hotel for Chinese officials only**		
开	kī **open**		
旅馆	léwgwān **hotel** (*standard Chinese hotel*)		
男厕(所)	nán tsèr(swǒr) **gents**		
女厕(所)	něw tsèr(swǒr) **ladies**		
三楼	sānló **third floor**		
上	shàrng **up**		
下	syà **down**		
小卖部	syǎomìbù **kiosk**		
闲人免进	syénrén myěnjìn **staff only**		

EATING OUT

bill
jàrngdān
账单

bowl
wǎn
碗

chopsticks
kwìdzir
筷子

dessert
tyénshír
甜食

drink
hēr
喝

eat
chīr
吃

food
shírwù
食物

menu
tsìpǔ
菜谱

restaurant
fàndyèn
饭店

salad
sèrlā
色拉

service
fúwù
服务

tea
chá
茶

waiter
jāodì
招待

waitress
jāodì
招待

water
shwǎy
水

a table for three, please
chíng jǎo ēejǎrng
sānrén jwōr·dzir
请找一张三人桌子

we'd like to order
wǒrmen syárng dyěn tsì
我们想点菜

what do you recommend?
něe twāy·jyèn shemmer?
你推荐什么？

I'd like ... please
wǒr yào ...
我要……

**can I have what he's
having?**
wǒr nérng yào éegèr hér
tā éeyàrng der tsì ma?
我能要一个和他一样
的菜吗？

19

EATING OUT

waiter/waitress!
jāodǐ!

招待！

could we have the bill, please?
wǒrmen kér·ee fùjàrng ma?

我们可以付账吗？

a pot of tea please
chǐng lí ēehú chá

请来一壶茶

tea with milk please
jyā nǐder chá

加奶的茶

that's for me
jèr shìr wór dyěn der

这是我点的

some more rice please
chǐng dzìlí ēesyěh měefàn

请再来一些米饭

a bottle of red wine/white wine please
chǐng lí ēepíng hóng pútáojyǒ/bí pútáojyǒ

请来一瓶红葡萄酒 /
白葡萄酒

chīngjēn fàndyèn **Muslim restaurant**	清真饭店	jyǒló **restaurant**	酒楼
fàndyèn **restaurant**	饭店	myèngwǎn **noodle shop**	面馆
fàngwǎn **restaurant**	饭馆	nán tsèr **gents**	男厕
hǐwày tsāngwǎn **seafood restaurant**	海味餐馆	něw tsèr **ladies**	女厕
jyǒjyā **restaurant**	酒家	sùtsìgwǎn **vegetarian restaurant**	素菜馆
		tsèrswǒr **toilet**	厕所

SOME BASIC MEATS

鸡	jēe **chicken**	猪肉	jūrò **pork**
牛肉	nyórò **beef**	肉	rò **meat (usually pork)**
鸭	yā **duck**		
鱼	yéw **fish**	羊肉	yárngrò **lamb**

RICE AND NOODLES

炒饭	chǎofàn **fried rice**	炒米粉	chǎoméefěn **fried rice noodles**
蛋炒饭	dàn chǎofàn **egg fried rice**	米饭	měefàn **rice**
面条	myèntyáo **noodles**	稀饭	syēefàn **rice porridge**

SOME BASIC MEALS AND FOOD ITEMS

包子	bāodzir **steamed dumplings with various fillings, normally including minced pork**

春卷	chūnjwǎrr **spring rolls**	豆腐干	dòfu gārr **dried bean curd**

豆腐乳	dòfu rǔ **fermented bean curd**
豆浆	dòjyārng **soya bean milk (typical breakfast drink)**
豆沙包	dòshābāo **steamed dumpling with sweet bean paste filling**

花卷	hwājwǎrr **steamed rolls**	馒头	mánto **steamed bread**

MENU READER

肉丸   ròwán
meatballs

咸菜   syéntsì
pickles

汤   tărng
soup

葱油饼   tsōngyóbǐng
spring onion pancake

油饼   yóbǐng
deep-fried savoury pancake

油条   yótyáo
savoury doughnut sticks (typical breakfast)

WAYS OF COOKING AND BASIC COMBINATIONS

炒⋯⋯   chăo . . .
stir-fried . . .

叉烧⋯⋯   chāshāo . . .
barbecued . . .

茄汁⋯⋯   chyéjīr . . .
. . . with tomato sauce

⋯⋯丁   . . . dīng
diced . . .

冬菇⋯⋯   dōnggū . . .
. . . with mushrooms

冬笋⋯⋯   dōngsŭn . . .
. . . with bamboo shoots

芙蓉⋯⋯   fúróng . . .
. . . with egg white

咖哩⋯⋯   gāli . . .
curried . . .

干烧⋯⋯   gānshāo . . .
. . . braised with chilli and bean sauce

宫保⋯⋯   gōngbăo . . .
stir-fried . . . with peanuts and chilli

蚝油⋯⋯   háoyó . . .
. . . with oyster sauce

红烧⋯⋯   hóngshāo . . .
. . . braised in brown (sweet and soya) sauce

MENU READER

滑溜......	hwályō ... **stir-fried ... with sauce**
火锅......	hwǒrgwōr ... **... fondue**
火腿......	hwórtwǎy ... **... with ham**
炸......	já ... **deep-fried ...**
榨菜......	jàtsì ... **... with pickled mustard greens**
鸡丁	jēedīng **diced chicken**
蒸......	jērng ... **steamed ...**
家常......	jyāchárng ... **home-style ...**
烤......	kǎo ... **roast ...**
......块	... kwìr **... chunks, pieces**
辣子......	làdzir ... **... with chilli**
麻酱......	májyàrng ... **... quick-fried in sesame paste**
麻辣......	málà ... **... with chilli and pepper**
木须......	mùsyēw ... **... with eggs, tree-ear (an edible fungus) and day lily (lily flowers dried for cooking)**
......片	... pyèrr **sliced ..., ... slices**
肉丝	ròsīr **shredded pork**
三鲜......	sānsyēn ... **'three-fresh' ... (with 3 particular ingredients varying from dish to dish)**
烧......	shāo ... **braised ...**
什锦......	shírjǐn ... **assorted ...**

23

MENU READER

时菜……	shírtsì …
	… with seasonal vegetables
……丝	… sīr
	shredded …
笋炒……	súnchǎo …
	stir-fried … with bamboo shoots
虾仁 ……	syárén …
	… with shrimps
虾仁·炒饭	syárén chǎofàn
	fried rice with shrimps
虾仁·炒面	syárén chǎomyèn
	fried noodles with shrimps
香酥 ……	syārngsū …
	crispy deep-fried …
蟹肉……	syèrò …
	… with crab
糖醋……	tárngtsù …
	sweet and sour …
葱爆……	tsōngbào …
	… quick-fried with spring onions
……丸	… wán
	… balls
鸭块	yākwǐr
	duck pieces
鱼片	yéwpyèrr
	fish slices
鱼香……	yéwsyārng …
	stir-fried … in hot spicy sauce
……元	… ywén
	… balls

COLD MEALS AS STARTERS

七彩冷拼盘	chēetsì lěrng pīnpárr
	'seven colours' cold platter
凤凰展翅	fèrnghwárng jǎnchìr
	'phoenix with spreading wings' cold platter
孔雀开屏	kǒngchwèh kīpíng
	'peacock plumage' cold platter

MENU READER

龙飞凤舞   lóngfāy fèrngwǔ
'dragon and phoenix dance' cold platter

六宝大拼盘   lyòbǎo dà pīnpárr
'six treasures' cold platter

三式拼盘   sānshìr pīnpárr
cold platter of three varieties of meat/vegetables

什锦拼盘   shírjǐn pīnpárr
mixed cold platter

五冷荤   wú lěrnghūn
cold platter of five varieties of meat/vegetables

PORK

板栗烧肉   bǎnlèe shāorò
pork braised with chestnuts

叉烧肉   chāshāo rò
barbecued pork

青椒炒肉片   chīngjyāo chǎo ròpyèrr
stir-fried sliced pork with green peppers

宫保肉丁   gōngbǎo ròdīng
stir-fried diced pork with peanuts and chilli

红烧蹄筋   hóngshāo téejìrr
pig's trotters braised in brown sauce

回锅肉   hwáygwōr rò
twice-cooked pork (first boiled then stir-fried)

滑溜肉片   hwályō ròpyèrr
stir-fried sliced pork with thick sauce

火锅猪排   hwǒrgwōr jūpí
pork chop fondue

榨菜炒肉丝   jàtsì chǎo ròsīr
stir-fried shredded pork with pickled mustard greens

酱爆三样   jyàrngbào sānyàrng
pork, pig's liver and kidneys quick-fried with bean sauce

米粉蒸肉   méefěn jērngrò
steamed pork with rice noodles

MENU READER

木须炒肉	mùsyēw chǎoròu **stir-fried sliced pork with eggs, tree-ear (edible fungus) and day lily (lily flower)**
肉丝炒饭 / 炒面	ròusīr chǎofàn/chǎomyèn **fried rice/noodles with shredded pork**
狮子头	shīrdzir tó **'lion head' (large meatball stewed with cabbage)**
时菜炒肉片	shírtsài chǎo ròupyèrr **stir-fried sliced pork with seasonal vegetables**
笋炒肉片	súnchǎo ròupyèrr **stir-fried sliced pork with bamboo shoots**
糖醋排骨	tárngtsù páigǔ **sweet and sour spareribs**
葱爆里脊	tsōngbào lěejēe **pork fillet quick-fried with spring onions**
鱼香肉丝	yéwsyārng ròusīr **stir-fried shredded pork in hot spicy sauce**

CHICKEN AND DUCK

北京烤鸭	Běyjīng kǎoyā **Peking duck**
白斩鸡	báijǎnjēe **sliced cold chicken in a hot spicy sauce**
茄汁鸡脯	chyéjīr jēepǔ **chicken breast with tomato sauce**
茄汁煎软鸭	chyéjīr jyēn rwǎnyā **fried duck with tomato sauce**
冬菇 / 冬笋鸡片	dōnggǔ/dōngsǔn jēepyèrr **chicken slices with mushrooms/bamboo shoots**
佛跳墙	fór tyào chyárng **'Buddha leaps the wall' (chicken with duck, pig's trotters and seafood stewed in rice wine)**
咖哩鸡块	gāli jēekwìr **curried chicken pieces**
宫保鸡丁	gōngbǎo·jēedīng **stir-fried diced chicken with peanuts and chilli**

26

MENU READER

怪味鸡	gwàiwàyrjēe **'strange-tasting chicken'** (whole chicken with peanuts and pepper)
红烧全鸭/全鸡	hóngshāo chwényā/chwénjēe **whole duck/chicken braised in brown sauce**
叫花鸡	jyàohwājēe **'beggar's chicken'** (charcoal-baked marinated chicken)
酱爆鸡丁	jyàrngbào jēedīng **diced chicken quick-fried with bean sauce**
酱爆鸭片菜心	jyàrngbào yāpyèrr tsìsyīn **sliced duck and green vegetables quick-fried with bean sauce**
樟茶鸭子	jārngchá yādzir **whole duck smoked with tea and camphor leaves**
辣子鸡丁	làdzir jēedīng **diced chicken with chilli**
珊瑚玉树鸡	shānhú yèwshù jēe **'coral and jade tree chicken'** (with crab or ham on vegetables)
时菜扒鸭	shírtsì páyá **braised duck with seasonal vegetables**
香酥鸭/鸡	syārngsū yā/jēe **crispy deep-fried whole duck/chicken**
葱爆烧鸭片	tsōngbào shāoyāpyèrr **sliced duck quick-fried with spring onions**

BEEF AND MUTTON

茄汁牛肉	chyéjir nyórò **stir-fried sliced beef with tomato sauce**
灯影牛肉	dērngyīng nyórò **'lamp shadow beef'** (spicy hot beef, finely sliced, steamed then deep-fried)
咖哩牛肉/羊肉	gāli nyórò/yárngrò **curried beef/mutton**
宫保牛肉	gōngbào nyórò **stir-fried beef with peanuts and chilli**

MENU READER

蚝油牛肉	háoyó nyóròu **stir-fried beef with oyster sauce**
红烧牛肉/羊肉	hóngshāo nyóròu/yárngròu **beef/mutton braised in brown sauce**
酱爆牛肉/羊肉	jyàrngbào nyóròu/yárngròu **beef/mutton quick-fried with bean sauce**
家常焖牛舌	jyāchárng mèn nyóshér **home-style braised ox tongue**
烤羊肉串	kǎo yárngròuchwàrr **kebabs**
麻酱牛肉	májyàrng nyóròu **beef quick-fried in sesame paste**
麻辣牛肉/羊肉	mála nyóròu/yárngròu **stir-fried beef/mutton with chilli and pepper**
时菜牛肉片/羊肉片	shírtsì nyóròupyèrr/ yárngròupyèrr **shredded beef/mutton with seasonal vegetables**
涮羊肉	shwàn yárngròu **Mongolian fondue**
笋炒牛肉	súnchǎo nyóròu **stir-fried beef with bamboo shoots**
葱爆牛肉/羊肉	tsōngbào nyóròu/yárngròu **beef/mutton quick-fried with spring onions**
鱼香牛肉	yéwsyārng nyóròu **stir-fried beef in hot spicy sauce**

FISH AND SEAFOOD

芙蓉虾仁	fúróng syārén **stir-fried shrimps with egg white**
咖哩鱿鱼	gāli yóyéw **curried squid**
干烧桂鱼	gānshāo gwàyyéw **Chinese perch braised with chilli and bean sauce**
干烧黄鳝	gānshāo hwárngshàn **eel braised with chilli and bean sauce**
红烧鲤鱼	hóngshāo lěeyéw **carp braised in brown sauce**

MENU READER

滑溜鱼片
hwályō yéwpyèrr
stir-fried fish slices with thick sauce

家常鱼块
jyāchárng yéwkwĭr
home-style fish

二吃大虾
lyǎrngchīr dàsyā
prawn heads deep-fried and bodies stir-fried

时菜虾球
shírtsì syāchyó
prawn balls with seasonal vegetables

虾仁干贝
syārén gānbày
scallops with shrimps

蟹肉鱼翅
syèrò yéwchìr
shark's fin with crab

糖醋鱼块
tárngtsù yéwkwĭr
sweet and sour fish

鱼香龙虾
yéwsyārng lóngsyā
stir-fried lobster in hot spicy sauce

SPECIALITIES

八宝饭
bābǎo fàn
'eight-treasure' rice pudding (with eight varieties of fruit and nuts)

叉烧包
chāshāobāo
steamed dumplings with barbecued pork fillings

锅贴
gwōrtyēh
fried Chinese ravioli

馄饨
húndūn
smaller Chinese ravioli in soup

蒸饺
jērng-jyǎo
steamed Chinese ravioli

家常豆腐
jyāchárng dòfu
home-style bean curd

麻辣豆腐
málà dòfu
bean curd with chilli and pepper

麻婆豆腐
mápór dòfu
bean curd with minced beef in hot spicy sauce

MENU READER

三鲜豆腐	sānsyēn dòfu **'three-fresh' bean curd made with three ingredients which vary**
三鲜水饺	sānsyēn shwáy-jyǎo **'three-fresh' Chinese ravioli ('three fresh' here usually means pork, shrimps and Chinese chives)**
砂锅豆腐	shāgwōr dòfu **bean curd in stew**
烧卖	shāomǐ **steamed dumplings open at the top, with sticky rice fillings**
水饺	shwáy-jyǎo **Chinese ravioli**
松花蛋	sōnghwādàn **preserved eggs**
小龙包	syǎolóngbāo **steamed dumplings with various fillings, served on the bamboo steamers in which they have been cooked**
虾仁豆腐	syārén dòfu **bean curd with shrimps**
鲜笋炒鸽片	syēnsǔn chǎo gērpyèrr **stir-fried pigeon slices with bamboo shoots**

VEGETABLES

菠菜炒鸡蛋	bōrtsǐ chǎo jēedàn **stir-fried spinach with eggs**
炒时菜	chǎo shírtsì **stir-fried seasonal vegetables**
冬菇菜心	dōnggū tsìsyīn **stir-fried oilseed rape with mushrooms**
冬笋扁豆	dōngsǔn byěndò **stir-fried French beans with bamboo shoots**
海米白菜	hǐměe bǐtsǐ **stir-fried Chinese cabbage with dried shrimps**
黄瓜炒鸡蛋	hwánggwā chǎo jēedàn **stir-fried cucumber with eggs**

MENU READER

菲菜炒鸡蛋
jyŏtsì chăo jēedàn
stir-fried Chinese chives with eggs

烧二冬
shāo èr dōng
stir-fried mushrooms and bamboo shoots with vegetables

素什锦
sù shírjĭn
stir-fried assorted vegetables

西红柿炒鸡蛋
syēehóngshìr chăo jēedàn
stir-fried tomato with eggs

鲜蘑豌豆
syēnmór wăndò
stir-fried peas with mushrooms

鱼香茄子
yéwsyărng chyédzir
stir-fried egg plant in hot spicy sauce

SOUPS *(eaten at the end of the meal)*

八宝冬瓜汤
bābăo dōnggwā tārng
'eight-treasure' winter marrow soup

紫菜汤
dzĭrtsì tārng
seaweed and dried shrimp soup

榨菜肉丝汤
jàtsì ròsìr tārng
soup with shredded pork and pickled mustard greens

竹笋鲜蘑汤
júsŭn syēnmór tārng
mushroom and bamboo shoot soup

木须汤
mùsyēw tārng
soup with sliced pork, eggs, tree-ear (an edible fungus) and day lily (lily flowers)

三鲜汤
sānsyēn tārng
'three-fresh' soup (normally prawns, a meat and a vegetable)

时菜肉片汤
shírtsì ròpyèrr tārng
pork and vegetable soup

酸辣汤
swān là tārng
hot and sour soup

西红柿鸡蛋汤
syēehóngshìr jēedàn tārng
egg and tomato soup

31

MENU READER

DESSERTS

扒丝苹果	básīr pínggwǒr **apple fritters**
扒丝山药	básīr shānyào **yam fritters**
扒丝香蕉	básīr syārng-jyāo **banana fritters**
冰糖银耳	bīngtárng yín'ěr **silver tree-ear in syrup (edible fungus)**
菠萝糯糟	bōrlwór láodzāo **pineapple in fermented glutinous rice**
莲子羹	lyéndzir gērng **lotus-seed in syrup**
三不粘	'sān bù jān' **'three non-stick' (dessert made from egg yolk, mung bean powder etc, – won't stick to your plate, chopsticks or teeth!)**
什锦水果羹	shírjǐn shwáygwǒr gērng **fruit salad**
杏仁豆腐	syìngrén dòufu **almond junket**
豌豆黄	wāndòuhwárng **sweet pea cake**

HAVING A DRINK

bar
jyŏbā
酒吧

beer
péejyŏ
啤酒

coke (R)
kérkŏkěrlèr
可口可乐

dry
gānder
干的

fresh orange
syīnsyēn jéwjīr
新鲜桔汁

gin and tonic
jīnjyŏ jyā
金酒加奎
kwáy·níngshwǎy
宁水

ice
bīng
冰

lemonade
níngmérng
chèeshwǎy
柠檬汽水

red wine
hóng pútáojyŏ
红葡萄酒

rice wine
mée jyŏ
米酒

straight (no ice)
bù jyā bīng
不加冰

sweet
tyénder
甜的

vodka
fútèrjyā
伏特加

whisky
wāyshìrjèe
威士忌

white wine
bí pútáojyŏ
白葡萄酒

wine
pútáojyŏ
葡萄酒

let's go for a drink
wŏmen chèw hēr dyǎr
shemmer ba
我们去喝点什么吧

a beer please
chīng lí ēebāy péejyŏ
请来一杯啤酒

two beers please
chīng lí lyǎrng bāy
péejyŏ
请来二杯啤酒

Chinese beer
Jōnggwór péejyŏ
中国啤酒

33

HAVING A DRINK

imported beer
jìnkǒ péejyǒ

进口啤酒

a glass of red wine/white wine
ēebāy hóng pútáojyǒ/bí pútáojyǒ

一杯红葡萄酒 /
白葡萄酒

can I try a Chinese spirit?
wǒr kér·ee lí ēedyar Jōnggwór lyèjyǒ ma?

我可以来一点中国
烈,酒吗？

with lots of ice
dwǒr jyā dyěn bīng

多加点,冰

no ice thanks
bú yào jyā bīng, syèh·syeh

不要加冰，谢谢

can I have another one?
wǒr kér·ee dzǐlí ēebāy ma?

我可以再来一杯吗？

the same again please
chīng lí ēeyàrng der

请来一样的

what'll you have?
née syǎrng hēr shemmer?

你想喝什么？

I'll get this round
jèr tsìr wǒr fùchyén

这次我付钱

not for me thanks
wǒr búyào, syèh·syeh

我不要，谢谢

he's absolutely smashed
tā fā jyǒ fērngler

他发酒疯了

34

HAVING A DRINK

茶馆   chágwăn **tea house** (*sometimes serving coffee*)

茶楼   cháló **teahouse** (*sometimes serving coffee*)

茶室   cháshìr **teahouse** (*sometimes serving coffee*)

酒吧   jyŏba **bar**

咖啡店   kāfāydyèn **café**

青岛啤酒   Qīngdăo píjiŭ (*R*) (*Chīngdăo péejyŏ*) **Qingdao beer**

崂山可乐   Láoshān kělè (*R*) (*Láoshān kěrlèr*) **Laoshan cola**

崂山矿泉水   Láoshān kuàng quán shuǐ (*R*) (*Láoshān kwàrng chwén shwǎy*) **Laoshan mineral water**

山楂酒   shānjājyŏ **liqueur made from berries**

杏仁霜   syìngrén·shwǎrng **non-alcoholic almond drink**

天府可乐   Tiānfú kělè (*R*) (*Tyēnfú kěrlèr*) **Tianfu cola**

五星啤酒   wŭxīng píjiŭ (*R*) (*wŭsyīng péejyŏ*) **five-star beer**

烟台味美思   Yāntái wèiměisī (*R*) (*Yēntí wàymǎysīr*) **Yantai vermouth**

音乐茶座   yīnyewèh cháxzwòr **tea and concert** (*live concerts of all types of music at a café or teahouse*)

COLLOQUIAL EXPRESSIONS

barmy
shǎmào
傻冒

bird
gū·nyárng
姑娘

bloke
syǎodzir
小子

nutter
yǒbìng
有病

pissed
shénjīng
syēesyēe der
神精兮兮的

thickie
bèndàn
笨蛋

twit
shǎgwā
傻瓜

great!
jēn bàrng!
真棒 !

that's awful!
jēn dzāogāo!
真糟糕 !

shut up!
hú shwōr
胡说 !

ouch!
ī yō!
哎哟 !

yum-yum!
hǎo syārng a!
好香啊 !

I'm absolutely knackered
wǒr lày·sirler
我累死了

I'm fed up
wǒr bú nǐfanler
我不耐烦了

I'm fed up with . . .
wǒr dwày . . . tǎoyèn
tòler
我对……讨厌透了

don't make me laugh!
byéh dò wǒr syào!
别逗我笑 !

COLLOQUIAL EXPRESSIONS

you've got to be joking!
nĕe bérng kĭ wánsyào!
你甭开玩笑！

it's rubbish (goods etc)
pòr wányìr
破玩意儿

it's a rip-off
chyāojúgàrng
敲竹杠

get lost!
gŭndàn!
滚蛋！

it's a damn nuisance
jēn tāmā der tăoyèn
真他妈的讨厌！

it's absolutely fantastic
jwéler
绝了！

别吹牛！
byéh chwāynyó!
don't boast!

大兵
dàbing
soldier(s)

还可以
híkér·ĕe
just so-so

真的！
jēnder!
I don't believe it!

老婆
lăopór
old lady, wife

老外
lăowì
foreigner(s)

聊天
lyáotyĕrr
to have a chat

神经病！
shénjīngbìng!
crazy!

他妈的！
tāmăder!
damn!, hell!

GETTING AROUND

bike
dzìr-syíngchēr
自行车

bus
gōnggòng
chèechēr
公共汽车

car
syǎo chèechēr
小汽车

change (*trains*)
hwànchēr
换车

chauffered car
lěw-yó chēr
旅游车

garage (*fuel,*
repairs) chèechēr
syōlěe chù
汽车修
理处

map
dèetú
地图

motorbike
mórtwōr-chēr
摩托车

pedicab
sānlúnchēr
三轮车

petrol
chèeyó
汽油

return (*air only*)
líhwáy-pyào
来回票

single (*air only*)
dānchérng-pyào
单程票

station
hwōrchērjàn
火车站

taxi
chūdzǔ chèechēr
出租汽车

ticket
chērpyào
车票

train
hwǒr-chēr
火车

tricycle
sānlúnchēr
三轮车

underground
dèetyěh
地铁

I'd like to rent a bike
wór syǎrng dzū
ěelyàrng dzìrsyíngchēr
我想租一辆自行车

how much is it per day?
ěetyēn dwǒrshao
chyén?
一天多少钱？

**when do I have to bring the
bike back?**
wǒr shemmer shírhò dáy
bǎ dzìr·syíngchēr
sònghwaylí?
我什么时候得把自
行车送回来？

GETTING AROUND

I'm heading for . . .
wǒr yào chèw . . .

我要去……

how do I get to . . .?
dào . . . dzémmer dzǒ?

到……怎么走 ?

REPLIES

一直朝前走

èejír cháochyén dzǒ
straight on

向左／右转

syàrng dzwór/yò jwǎn
turn left/right

就是那幢房子

jyò shìr nà jwàrng fárng·dzir
it's that building there

从那条路往回走

tsóng nà tyáo lù wǎrng·hwáydzǒ
it's back that way

左边的第一／第二／第三个

dzwǒrbyēn der dèe ēe/dèe èr/dèe sān·ger
first/second/third on the left

we're just travelling around
wǒrmen jǐr shìr dzi jèr ēe dì gwàrng·gwarng

我们只是在这一带逛逛

I'm a stranger here
jèrger dèefārng wǒr bùshú

这个地方我不熟

is that on the way?
nà jyò dzì yào jìnggwòr der lùshàrng ma?

那就在要经过的路上吗 ?

can I get off here?
wǒr kér·ee dzì jèrlee syàchèr ma?

我可以在这里下车吗？

39

GETTING AROUND

thanks for the lift
syèh·syeh něe kīchēr
sòng wŏr

谢谢你开车送我

two tickets to . . . please
chíng mǐ lyǎrng jǎrng
chèw . . . der pyào

请买两张去……
的票

**a ticket for tomorrow
please**
chíng mǐ ēejǎrng
míngtyēn der pyào

请买一张明天的票,

**what time is the last train
back?**
dzwày mòr ēebān
hwǒrchēr shemmer
shírhò hwáylí?

最末一班火车什么时
候回来?

can I use this ticket?
wŏr kér·ee yòng jèrjǎrng
pyào ma?

我可以用这张票吗?

**can I have a refund for this
ticket?**
wŏr kér·ee twày jèrjǎrng
pyào ma?

我可以退这张票吗?

can I change this ticket?
wŏr kér·ee hwàn
ēejǎrng pyào ma?

我可以换一张票吗?

**is this the right platform for
. . .?**
jèr shìr dào . . . der jàntí
ma?

这是到……的站
台吗?

is this train going to . . .?
jèr shìr chèw . . . der
hwǒrchēr ma?

这是去……的火
车吗?

40

GETTING AROUND

where are we?
jèr shìr nǎrr?

这是哪儿？

which stop is it for . . .?
dào . . . dzǐ nǎ ēejàn
syàchēr?

到……在哪一站
下车？

can I take my bike on the train?
wǒr kér·ee bǎ
dzìr·syíngchēr dǐ shàrng
hwǒrchēr ma?

我可以把自行车带
上火车吗？

how far is it to the nearest petrol station?
dào dzwày·jìn der
jyā·yójàn yǒ
dwǒr·yewěn?

到最近的加油站
有多远？

I need a new tyre
wǒr syēw·yào ēejir
syīnlúntī

我需要一只新轮胎

it's overheating
mǎdá tī rèrler

马达太热了

there's something wrong with the brakes
shāchēr yǒ máobìng

刹车有毛病

汽车加油站	chèechēr jyāyójàn **petrol station**	起飞时间	chēefǎy shírjyēn **flight departure time(s)**
汽车修理厂	chèechēr syōléechǎrng **garage, repair shop**	请勿吸烟	chīng wù syēeyēn **no smoking please**

41

GETTING AROUND

出租汽车	chūdzū chèechēr **taxi**	禁止通行	jìnjǐr tōngsyíng **road closed**
出租自行车	chūdzū dzìrsyíngchēr **bicycles for hire**	检票口	jyěnpyàokǒ **ticket barrier**
出站口	chūjànkǒ **arrivals**	老人孕妇专座	lǎorén yèwnfù jwǎndzwòr **reserved for the elderly and pregnant women**
前面施工	chyénmyèn shīrgōng **roadworks ahead**		
单行线	dānsyíng syèn **one-way traffic**	列车到站 时刻表	lyèchē dàojàn shírkèrbyǎo **train arrival time(s)**
地铁	dèetyěh **underground**	人行横道	rénsyíng hérngdào **pedestrian crossing**
陡坡	dǒpōr **steep hill**		
一慢 二看 三 通过	ēemàn èrkàn sāntōnggwòr **first slow down, second look, third cross**	售票处	shòupyàochù **ticket office**
		小心路滑	syāosyīn lùhwá **take care, slippery road surface**
火车站	hwǒrchērjàn **station**		
站台票	jàntípyào **platform tickets**	通宵车	tōngsyāochēr **all-night bus**
禁区	jìnchēw **restricted area**	此路不通	tsǐrlùbùtōng **dead end**
进站口	jìnjànkǒ **departures**	铁路道口	tyělùdàokǒ **level crossing**
禁止驶入	jìnjǐr shǐrù **no entry**	问讯处	wènsyèwnchù **enquiries**
禁止停车	jìnjǐr tíngchēr **no parking**	5号码头	wǔhào mǎtó **dock number 5**

SHOPPING

carrier bag
sùlyàodì
塑料袋

cashdesk
shōkwāntí
收款白

cheap
pyénee
便宜

cheque
jirpyào
支票

department
gwàytí
柜台

expensive
gwày
贵

market
shārngchǎrng
商场

pay
fùkwǎn
付款

receipt
shōjèw
收据

shop
shārng·dyèn
商店

shop assistant
shò·hwòr·yewén
售货员

supermarket
chāojée
shìrchǎrng
超级市场

I'd like ...
wǒr yào ...
我要……

have you got ...?
yǒ ... ma?
有……吗?

how much is this?
jèr dwōrshao chyén?
这多少钱?

the one in the window
dzì chú·chwārng·lee
nà·éegèr
在橱窗里那一个

do you take credit cards?
němen jyēshò syìnyòng
kǎ ma?
你们接受信用卡吗?

**could I have a receipt
please?**
kér·ee gáy wǒr ēejārng
shōjèw ma?
可以给我一张收据
吗?

43

SHOPPING

I'd like to try it on
wór syăng shìrshir

我想试试

I'll come back
wŏr hwày dzìli

我会再来

it's too big/small
tì dàler/syăoler

太大了／小了

it's not what I'm looking for
jèr bú shìr wór syăng·yào der

这不是我想要的

I'll take it
wór mĭsyàler

我买下了

can you gift-wrap it?
nĕe nérng tèe wŏr băojwărng éesyà ma?

你能替我包装一下吗？

bĭhwòr dàló
department store

百货大楼

bĭhwòr gōngsīr
department store

百货公司

bĭhwòr shărngdyèn
department store

百货商店

chūkŏ
exit

出口

dà jyĕnjyà
sale

大减价

gùkèr jĭrbù
no admission to customers

顾客止步

jyáokwănchù
cash point

缴款处

rùkŏ
entrance

入口

shírpĭn shărngdyèn
food store

食品商店

shōkwăntí
cash point

收款台

syénrén myĕnjìn
staff only

闲人免进

wénwù shărngdyèn
antique shop

文物商店

yíngyèh shírjyèn
opening hours

营业时间

44

SIGHTSEEING AND ENTERTAINMENT

Great Wall
The 'Chángchéng' is over 5000 kilometres long, crossing China from east to west as a defence against the northern nomads. The great emperor Qín Shǐhuáng linked earlier sections and completed the wall in the 3rd century BC.

Forbidden City
The 'Zǐjìnchéng' or grand palace in Beijing where the ancient Chinese emperors lived. Today it houses the National Palace Museum.

Terra Cotta Army
The 'bīngmáyǒng' is a lifesize model army guarding the tomb of emperor Qín Shǐhuáng since the 3rd century BC (this emperor was responsible for unifying the Chinese written language, legal and measurement systems).

Chinese Opera
This is one of the most popular forms of entertainment, with countless regional varieties, one of the best known being Beijing Opera or 'jīngjù'. Go to a park on a Saturday morning and you'll see crowds of (older) people playing traditional Chinese musical instruments and singing Beijing Opera.

Taìjí
Also known as 'shadow boxing', this is like a type of slow-motion aerobics and is very popular with older people. You will often see people doing taìjí in public parks, especially before breakfast.

45

CHINA AND THINGS CHINESE

GETTING AROUND

Two important points: 1. train travel is very popular, but there are no return tickets; 2. your ticket will only be valid on the train leaving at the time printed on it. Refunds (for which there is a small fee) are possible if application is made in good time. Train services (especially long-distance ones) are not that frequent, so missing a train could mean a delay of a day or so.

FESTIVALS

Chinese New Year
This is the most important Chinese festival, also known as the Spring Festival or 'chūnjié'. It is based on the lunar calendar and the date varies each year between the end of January and the middle of February. Celebrations usually continue for three days during which time families get together for sumptuous dinners. The climax of the festival is on New Year's Eve when, as the New Year's bell rings, people let off fireworks.

Lantern Festival
'Yuánxiāo jié', with dazzling displays of coloured lanterns of all shapes and sizes, is held at the first full moon after Chinese New Year and marks the end of the New Year celebrations. Typical festival food is 'tāngyuán', a sweet dumpling made of sticky rice pastry.

Dragon Boat Festival
'Duānwǔ jié', held on the 5th day of the 5th lunar month, commemorates the ancient poet and official Qū Yuán who drowned himself in protest at official corruption. Dragon boat races are held in his honour. 'Zòngzǐ' or rice balls wrapped in leaves are thrown into the water to appease the dragons there.

CHINA AND THINGS CHINESE

Mid-autumn Moon Festival
'Zhōngqiū jié', held on the 15th night of the 8th
lunar month at full moon, is a traditional festival
celebrating the importance of family ties. Members of a
family, especially if separated, eat 'moon cake' or
'yuèbǐng' and make a wish that one day the family
may be together again, complete like the full moon.

National Day
October 1st — commemorates the founding of the
People's Republic in 1949.

GEOGRAPHICAL

Yangtse River
Known as the 'Long River' or 'Chángjiāng', this is
the longest river in China, rising on the Tibetan
plateau and flowing into the East China Sea at
Shanghai.

Yangtse Gorges
The 'Chángjiāng sānxiá' - a famous and
spectacular scenic area in the middle reaches of the
Yangtse River.

Here is a list of some of the main Chinese tourist
cities, with their names written in Chinese characters
and in Pinyin:

北京　　**Běijīng (Báyjīng)**
the capital of China

上海　　**Shànghǎi (Shàrnghǐ)**
China's largest city and one of the most
industrially developed

CHINA AND THINGS CHINESE

杭州 **Hángzhōu (Hárngjō)**
south of Shanghai, site of the famous
West Lake or Xīhú (Syeēhú)

苏州 **Sūzhōu (Sūjō)**
small city near Shànghǎi, famous for its
gardens

无锡 **Wúxī (Wúsyēe)**
lots of typical Chinese pavilions and pagodas

西安 **Xīān (Syēe-ān)**
ancient capital city in north central China

桂林 **Guìlín (Gwàylín)**
busy tourist city in south-west China, set
among spectacular limestone hills

ADDRESSING PEOPLE

In addition to the forms for Mr/Mrs etc as given in the
dictionary in this book, Chinese also address each
other by using the surname prefixed by either 'lǎo' or
'xiǎo' (syǎo). You can imitate this style if you want
to be friendly and informal. If you think someone is
over 40, use 'lǎo' (which means old) and if you think
someone is under 40 use 'xiǎo' (which means young)
– for example you would address Mr or Mrs or Miss
Wang as:

          lǎo Wáng
or   xiǎo Wáng

Most Chinese have three-character names. The first is
the surname and the other two the names chosen by
the parents.

CHINA AND THINGS CHINESE

EATING

Most Chinese restaurants will give you chopsticks. It is
quite in order to lift the bowl up to your mouth and use
the chopsticks to push the food into your mouth.
When you put your chopsticks down, lay them across
the bowl. Don't stick them upright in the bowl, this
looks like a temple-offering!

Eating in China is a major cultural activity. Meals are
relaxed, with few 'do's' and 'don'ts'. It is only essential
to enjoy yourself.

At the beginning of the meal, the host may apologize
for the 'meagre spread'. You should not agree, but can
contradict him, perhaps by saying 'hén hǎo!', hén
hǎo' (very good). He will then invite the guests to
start.

It is a good thing to make appreciative comments like
'hǎo chī!, hǎo chī!' (hǎo chīr, hǎo chīr — delicious,
delicious) but often best not to enquire what
you are eating. It is polite to have plenty, and you can
watch the host and the other guests so as not to finish
too fast.

When there are toasts, you hold the glass out in front
of you. Though 'gānbēi' (gānbāy) means 'dry
glass', a sip is fine.

If someone pours you a drink (including tea) it is polite
to hold the cup or glass in both hands.

Towards the end of the meal, guests who have
finished may say 'màn chī' (màn chīr — slow eat).
This means 'I've finished, but please don't hurry'.
The host may press you to take some more. If you've
had enough to eat, you could say something like
'zhēn bǎole xièxiè' (jēn bǎoler syèh-syeh — I'm
really satisfied, thank you).

There is never coffee at the end of a Chinese meal
(though jasmine tea is often drunk). When the eating
is over in a restaurant the guests go home.

CHINA AND THINGS CHINESE

LANGUAGE

There are many Chinese dialects, especially in the
south, and though very similar in structure, they are
often unintelligible outside the district where they are
spoken. The Mandarin dialect of north China was
chosen this century as the standard language
(pūtōnghuà).

Written Chinese is the same throughout the whole
country. In the People's Republic many characters
have been modified and the script is written from left
to right, as in European languages. In Hong Kong and
Taiwan the traditional characters have been retained
and are still often written in columns, from top to
bottom, right to left.

Some characters are derived from pictures:

竹　　　　**bamboo**

马　　　　**horse**

人　　　　**man, person**

Some are a combination of pictures:

明　　　　**bright (a sun 日 and a moon 月)**

好　　　　**good (a woman 女 and a child 子)**

But most characters are made up of a 'sense part' (the
radical) and a 'sound part' (the phonetic). The character
for 'copper':

铜　　　　(pronounced 'tóng')

　　　　　combines the metal radical 钅

　　　　　with the phonetic 同 tóng.

CHINA AND THINGS CHINESE

The character for 'oil':

油   ('yóu' – pronounced yó)

combines the water radical 氵

with the phonetic 由 yó

Chinese is a tonal language (see Introduction). The same syllable will have completely different meanings differentiated only by tone. For example:

妈	**mā** mother	马	**mǎ** horse
麻	**má** hemp	骂	**mà** tell off

CHINESE MEASUREMENT SYSTEM

China has some special measurements for everyday usage:

1 丈 zhàng (jàrng) = 10 尺 chǐ (chǐr) = 3.33 metres

1 尺 chǐ (chǐr) = 10 寸 cùn (tsùn) = 0.33 metres

1 里 (lǐ) = 500 metres

1 斤 (jīn) = 10 两 liǎng (lyǎrng) = 0.5 kilos

MONEY

bank
yínhárng
银行

bill
jàrngdān
账单

bureau de change
wìhwày
dwày·hwànchù
外汇兑
换处

change (*small*)
língchyén
零钱

cheque
jīrpyào
支票

credit card
syìnyòng kǎ
信用卡

exchange rate
hwày·dwàylèw
汇兑率

expensive
gwày
贵

foreign exchange certificate
wìhwày·jwèn
外汇券

pounds (sterling)
yīngbàrng
英镑

price
jyàgér
价格

traveller's cheque
lěw·syíng
jīrpyào
旅行支票

how much is it?
jèr dwōrshao chyén?
这多少钱？

I'd like to change this into ...
wór syáng bǎ tā
hwàncherng ...
我想把它换成 ......

can you give me something smaller?
něe nérng gǎy ēesyēh
língchyén ma?
你能给一些零钱吗？

can I use this credit card?
wǒr nérng yòng jèrjǒng
syìnyòng kǎ ma?
我能用这种信用卡吗？

can we have the bill please?
wǒrmen kér·ee fùkwǎn ma?
我们可以付款吗？

please keep the change
chīng lyósyà língchyén
请留下零钱

52

MONEY

does that include service?
jèrger jyàchyén bāokwòr
fúwùfày ma?

这个价钱包括服务费吗？

I think the figures are wrong
wŏr jwéder shùdzìr
tswòrler

我觉得数字错了

I'm completely skint
wŏr ēefēn
chyén yĕh máy yŏ

我一分钱也没有

Chinese currency is known as 'Rénmínbì'. The unit is the 'yuán' (*yew·én*) which is equal to ten 'jiăo' (*jyăo*) or 100 'fēn' (*fēn*). In spoken Chinese, however, a 'yuán' is called a 'kuài' (*kwì*) and a 'jiăo' is called a 'máo'. As a foreigner you will also change money into foreign exchange certificates (*FECs*) for use in tourist shops and hotels.

yuán yew·én	元	
jiăo jyăo	角	
fēn fēn	分	
kuài kwì	块	
máo máo	毛	

Jŏnggwór
rénmín
yínhárng
People's Bank of China (*dealing only with domestic currency*)

中国人民
银行

rénmínbèe
name for Chinese currency (*shortened to RMB*)

人民币

Jŏnggwór
yínhárng
Bank of China (*dealing with foreign currency*)

中国银行

wĭhwày
dwàyhwàn
foreign exchange

外汇兑换

53

ENTERTAINMENT

band (*pop*)
yewèh·dwày   乐队

Beijing Opera
jīngjèw   京剧

cinema
dyènyīng·yewèn   电影院

classical music
gúdyěn
yīn·yewèh   古典音乐

concert
yīn·yewèh
hwày   音乐会

disco
déesīrkēr   迪斯科

film
dyènyīng   电影

folk music
mínjyēn
yīn·yewèh   民间音乐

go out
chūchèw·wán   出去玩

music
yīn·yewèh   音乐

play (*theatre*)
syèejèw   戏剧

pop music
tōngsú
yīn·yewèh   通俗音乐

rock music
yáogǔn·yewèh   摇滚乐

seat
dzwòrwày   座位

show
yěnchū   演出

singer
gērchàrng·jyā   歌唱家
(*pop*)
gērsyīng   歌星

theatre
jèw·yewèn   剧院

ticket
pyào   票

are you doing anything tonight?
něe jīnwán yǒ shìr ma?   你今晚有事吗？

do you want to come out with me tonight?
něe jīnwán syǎrng hér wǒr èechēe chūchèw ma?   你今晚想和我一起出去吗？

54

ENTERTAINMENT

what's on?
yĕn shemmer?

演什么？

have you got a programme of what's on in town?
née yŏ chérnglee dzwày·jìn der jyémù yĕnchū rìr·chérng·byăo ma?

你有城里最近的节目演出日程表吗？

which is the best disco round here?
jèr fùjìn nă·ēe·jyā déesīrkēr wúchărng dzwày hăo?

这附近哪一家迪斯科舞场最好？

let's go to the cinema/theatre
wŏrmen chèw kàn dyànyĭng/syèejèw ba

我们去看电影／戏剧吧

I've seen it
wór ēejīng kàn·gwórler

我已经看过了

I'll meet you at 9 o'clock at the station
wŏr jyódyĕn dzì chērjàn dérng nĕe

我九点在车站等你

can I have two tickets for tonight's performance?
wŏr nérng mí lyărng·jàrng jīnwăn yĕnchū der pyào ma?

我能买二张今晚演出的票吗？

I'd like to book three seats for tomorrow
wór syărng yèwdìng míngtyēn der sān·ger dzwòrwày

我想预订明天的三个座位

do you want to dance?
née syărng tyàowŭ ma?

你想跳舞吗？

55

ENTERTAINMENT

do you want to dance again?
née syǎrng dzì tyào éetsìr ma?

你想再跳一次吗？

thanks but I'm with my boyfriend
syèh·syèhler, wǒr hér wǒr nánpérng·yǒ dzì·èechēe

谢谢了，我和我男朋友在一起

let's go out for some fresh air
wǒrmen chūchèw hwànhwàn syīnsyēn kōngchèe ba

我们出去换换新鲜空气吧

will you let me back in again later?
gwòr ēehway·r něe hí hwày ràrng wǒr jìnlí ma?

过一会儿你还会让我进来吗？

电影院	dyènyǐng·yewèn **cinema**	台球	tíchyó **pool room**
剧场	jèwchǎrng **theatre**	影剧院	yīngjèw·yewèn **theatre**
客满	kèrmǎn **house full**		

BUSINESS

business shēng·èe	生意	**managing director** jīnglěe	经理
business card míngpyèn	名片	**meeting** hwàyèe	会议
company gōngsir	公司	**price** jyàgér	价格
contract hértóng	合同	**quote** (*noun*) kījyà	开价
fax (*noun*) chwánjēn	传真	**target** jǐrbyāo	指标
instalment fēnchēe fùkwǎn	分期付款	**telex** dyènchwán	电传
invoice fāpyào	发票	**workflow schedule** gōngdzwòr jìnchéng·byǎo	工作进程表

I have a meeting with Mr... wǒr yào jyèn ... syēnshēng	我要见……先生
may I introduce Mr ...? wǒr kér·ee jyèh·shào ... syēnshēng ma?	我可以介绍…… 先生吗？
he is our technical director/sales director tā shìr wǒrmender jèeshù jīnglěe/ twǎysyāo jīnglěe	他是我们的技术 经理／推销经理

BUSINESS

can we send you faxes in English?
wŏrmen nérng yòng Yīng·yĕw gáy nĕemen fā chwánjĕn ma?

我们能用英语给你们发传真吗？

I'd like to have time to think it over
ràrng wŏr kăolèw éesyà ba

让我考虑一下吧

we're very excited about it
wŏrmen dwày jèr hén găn syìngchèw

我们对这很感兴趣

I'm afraid this is still a problem
kŏngpà jèr réngrán shir éegèr wèntee

恐怕这仍然是一个问题

ok, that's a deal
hăo ba, chéng jyāoler

好吧,成交了

excellent!
tì hăoler

太好了！

let's drink to a successful partnership
wày wŏrmender chénggōng hérdzwòr gānbăy

为我们的成功合作干杯！

it's a pleasure doing business with you
hér nĕemen dzwòr shēng·èe fāycháng yéwkwĭl

和你们做生意非常愉快.

PROBLEMS

accident shìrgù	事故	**fire brigade** syāofárng·dwày	消防队
ambulance jyòhùchēr	救护车	**ill** shērngbìngler	生病了
broken hwiler	坏了	**injured** shòshārng	受伤
doctor ēeshērng	医生	**late** chírdào	迟到
emergency jéeshir	急事	**out of order** chū gùjàrng	出故障
fire hwŏrdzĭ	火灾	**police** jīngchá	警察

can you help me? I'm lost
nĕe nérng bārng ger
márng ma? wŏr mée lù ler

你能帮个忙吗？
我迷路了

I've lost my passport
wŏr hùjào dyōler

我护照丢了

**I've locked myself out of
my room**
wŏr chūmén wàrngler dì
yàoshir

我出门忘了带钥匙

my luggage hasn't arrived
wŏr syínglĕe hí máy
dào

我行李还没到

I can't get it open
wór dă bù kī

我打不开

it's jammed
kă jùler

卡住了

59

PROBLEMS

I don't have enough money
wŏrder chyén búgòu
我的钱不够

I've broken down
wŏrder chēr hwǐler
我的车坏了

this is an emergency
wór yŏ jéeshìr
我有急事

help!
jyòmìng!
救命！

it doesn't work
jèr dōngsyee hwǐler
这东西坏了

the lights aren't working in my room
wŏr fárng·jyēn der dērng hwǐler
我房间的灯坏了

the lift is stuck
dyèntēe gáy kǎjùler
电梯给卡住了

I can't understand a single word
wŏr éegèr dzìr yěh tīngbùdŏng
我一个字也听不懂

can you get an interpreter?
nĕe nérng jăo éegèr fānèe ma?
你能找一个翻译吗？

the toilet won't flush
tsèrswŏr máyfă chōngshwǎy ler
厕所没法冲水了

there's no plug in the bath
yèwchírlĕe máy yŏ sĭdzir
浴池里没有塞子

there's no hot water
máy yŏ rèrshwǎy
没有热水

there's no toilet paper left
máy yŏ shójĭr ler
没有手纸了

60

PROBLEMS

I'm afraid I've accidentally broken the . . .
hĕn bàochyèn wŏr bù
syăosyīn nòng·hwĭler . . .

很报歉我不小心
弄坏了……

this man has been following me
jèr·rén èejír gēnjer wŏr

这人一直跟着我

I've been mugged
wŏr bày chyărng·jyéler

我被抢劫了

my handbag has been stolen
wŏrder shŏtéebāo bày
tōler

我的手提包被偷了

公安局	gōng·ānjéw **Public Security Bureau** (*Chinese police station*)	消防队	syāofárngdwày **fire brigade**
		小心！	syāosyīn! **caution!**
急诊室	jéejĕnshìr **first-aid room**	太平门	tĭpíngmén **emergency exit**
警察	jīngchá **police**	危险！	wāysyĕn! **danger!**
禁止……	jìnjĭr . . . **. . . forbidden**		
救护车	jyòhùchēr **ambulance**		
灭火器	myèh·hwŏrchèe **fire extinguisher**		

61

acupuncture jēnjyŏ	针灸	**disabled** tsánjeeder	残疾的
bandage bērngdì	绷带	**disease** bìng	病
blood syew·èh	血	**doctor** ēeshērng	医生
broken pèrngshārng	碰伤	**health** jyènkārng	健康
burn shāoshārng	烧伤	**hospital** ēe·yewèn	医院
chemist's yàofárng	药房	**ill** shērngbìngler	生病了
contraception bèeyèwn	避孕	**nurse** hùshir	护士
dentist yákēr ēeshērng	牙科医生	**wound** shārngkǒ	伤口

I don't feel well
wǒr jwéder shēntēe bù shūfu

我觉得身体不舒服

it's getting worse
bìngchíng dzì jyājòng

病情在加重

I feel better
wǒr jwéder hǎosyeler

我觉得好些了

I feel sick
wǒr jwéder hwày tù

我觉得会吐

I've got a pain here
wǒr jèrr térng

我这儿疼

it hurts
tòng

痛

HEALTH

he's got a temperature
tā fāshāoler

他发烧了

could you call a doctor?
něe nérng chǐng ēesherng ma?

你能请医生吗？

is it serious?
bìngchíng yénjòng ma?

病情严重吗？

will he need an operation?
tā syēw·yào dzwòr shǒshù ma?

他需要做手术吗？

I'm diabetic
wór yǒ tárng·nyàobìng

我有糖尿病

have you got anything for …?
née yǒ jìr … der yào ma?

你有治……的药吗？

chěwyào **dispensary**	取药	kōchyārngkēr **dental department**	口腔科
ēe·yewèn **hospital**	医院	nàykēr **medical department**	内科
ěrbéehókēr **ENT department**	耳鼻喉科	péefūkēr **dermatology**	皮肤科
fùchǎnkēr **gynaecology and obstetrics**	妇产科	syǎoérkēr **paediatrics**	小儿科
gwàhào **registration**	挂号	wìbīn ménjěnbù **foreign out-patients**	外宾门诊部
jéejěnshìr **emergency**	急诊室	yěnkēr **eye department**	眼科
Jōng ēekēr **Chinese medicine department**	中医科		

63

SPORT

can we play table-tennis?
wŏmen kér·ee dă
pīngpārngchyó ma?

我们可以打乒乓
球吗？

I'm going jogging
wŏr yào chèw păobù

我要去跑步

I'd like to learn to ice-skate
wór syărng syew·éh hwábīng

我想学滑冰

**how about a game of
badminton?**
chèw dă ēehway·r
yĕwmáochyó
dzěmmeryàrng?

去打一会儿羽毛
球怎么样？

can we use the tennis court?
wŏmen kér·ee yòng
wărng·chyó·chărng ma?

我们可以用网球场吗？

**we want to go on a bicycle
trip**
wŏmen syárng găo ger
chéechěr lěw·yó

我们想搞个骑车旅游

**I'd like to go and watch a
basketball match**
wór syărng chèw kàn
ēechărng lánchyósì

我想去看一场篮球赛

**can I do shadow-boxing
(taichi) with you?**
wŏr kér·ee hér nĕe
èechēe dă tìjéechwén ma?

我可以和你一起打
太极拳吗？

**this is the first time I've
ever tried it**
jèr shìr wŏr dèe·ēetsìr
shìrjer wán jèrger

这是我第一次试着
玩这个

64

letter
syìn
信

send
jìe
寄

parcel
bāogwŏr
包裹

stamp
yóupyào
邮票

post office
yójéw
邮局

telegram
dyènbào
电报

registered
gwàhàosyìn
挂号信

how much is a letter to Ireland?
jìe dào ì·ěrlán der syìn dwŏrshǎo chyén?

寄到爱尔兰的信多
少钱？

I'd like four '1 yuan 6 jiao' stamps
wór syárng mǐ sìr jārng ēeyewén lyòjyǎo der yópyào

我想买四张一元六角
的邮票

I'd like six stamps for postcards to England
wór syárng mǐ lyò jārng wǎrng Yīng·gwór jìe míng·syìnpyèn der yópyào

我想买六张往英国
寄名信片的邮票

is there any mail for me?
yó wŏrder syìn ma?

有我的信吗？

I'm expecting a parcel from ...
wŏr dzì děrng éegèr tsóng ... lí der bāogwŏr

我在等一个人……
来的包裹

65

THE POST OFFICE

can I send this express?
wŏr nérng jèe tèkwì ma?

我能寄特快吗？

can I send this airmail?
wŏr nérng jèe
hárngkōng ma?

我能寄航空吗？

包裹，印刷品	bāogwŏr, yìnshwāpĭn **parcels, printed matter**	开箱时间	kīsyärng shírjyēn **collection times**
长途电话	chárngtú dyènhwà **long-distance telephones**	营业时间	yíngyèh shírjyēn **opening hours**
电报	dyènbào **telegrams**	邮票，挂号	yópyào, gwàhào **stamps, registered mail**

directory enquiries cháhàotí	查号台	**operator** dzŏngjēe	总机
engaged jànsyèn	占线	**phone** (*verb*) dǎ dyènhwà	打电话
extension fēnjēe	分机	**phone box** dyènhwàtíng	电话亭
number dyènhwà hàoma	电话号码	**telephone** dyènhwà	电话

is there a phone round here?
jèr fùjìn yǒ dyènhwà ma?

这附近有电话吗？

can I use your phone?
wǒr kér·ee yòng něeder dyènhwà ma?

我可以用你的电话吗？

I'd like to make a phone call to Britain
wór syárng wǎrng Yīng·gwór dǎ ger dyènhwà

我想往英国打个电话

I want to reverse the charges
wór syǎrng ràrng dwàyfārng fùkwǎn

我想让对方付款

hello
wày

喂

67

TELEPHONING

could I speak to Li?
chíng jǎo·éesyà Lěe
syēnshērng

请找一下李先生

hello, this is Simon speaking
wày, wǒr shìr 'Simon'

喂，我是 Simon

can I leave a message?
wǒr kér·ee lyó ger
kǒsyìn ma?

我可以留个口信吗？

do you speak English?
née jyǎrng Yīngyěw
ma?

你讲英语吗？

could you say that again very very slowly?
něe kér·ee fāychárng
fāychárng màander dzì
shwǒr ēebyèn ma?

你可以非常非常慢
地再说一遍吗？

could you tell him Jim called?
něe nérng gàosu tā 'Jim'
dǎgwòr dyènhwà ma?

你能告诉他 Jim
打过电话吗？

could you ask her to ring me back?
něe nérng chīng tā gáy
wǒr hwáy ger dyènhwà
ma?

你能请他给我回
个电话吗？

I'll call back later
wǒr gwòr ēehway·r dzì
dǎ gwòrll

我过一会儿再打过来

my number is . . .
wǒrder dyènhwà hàoma
shìr . . .

我的电话号码是……

76 32 11
chēe lyò sān èr yāo
yāo

七六三二一一

68

TELEPHONING

just a minute please
chíng děrng ēehway·r

请等一会儿

he's not in
tā bú dzì

他不在

sorry, I've got the wrong number
dwàybuchěe, wór gǎotswòrler hàoma

对不起，我搞错了号码

it's a terrible line
jèr dyènhwà hěn bù chīngchu

这电话很不清楚

REPLIES

嗯

wày
hello

请等会儿

chíng dérng hwǎy·r
hang on

你是谁呀？

něe shìr sháy ya?
who's calling?

查号台	cháhàotí **directory enquiries**	公用电话	gōngyòng dyènhwà **public telephone**
长途电话	chárngtú dyènhwà **long-distance telephone**	火警、盗警、匪警	hwórjǐng, dàojǐng, fáyjǐng **09 – emergency number for fire, burglary and robbery**
电话簿	dyènhwàbù **telephone directory**		
一次四分	éetsìr sìrfēn **four fen per call**		

NUMBERS, THE DATE, THE TIME

0 líng	零	16 shírlyò	十六
1 ēe	一	17 shírchēe	十七
2 èr (but lyǎrng for time)	二	18 shírbā	十八
3 sān	三	19 shírjyǒ	十九
4 sìr	四	20 èrshír	二十
5 wǔ	五	21 èrshír·ēe	二十一
6 lyò	六	22 èrshír·èr	二十二
7 chēe	七	30 sānshír	三十
8 bā	八	35 sānshírwǔ	三十五
9 jyǒ	九	40 sìrshír	四十
10 shír	十	50 wǔshír	五十
11 shír·ēe	十一	60 lyòshír	六十
12 shír·èr	十二	70 chēeshír	七十
13 shírsān	十三	80 bāshír	八十
14 shírsìr	十四	90 jyǒshír	九十
15 shírwǔ	十五	91 jyǒshír·ēe	九十一

NUMBERS, THE DATE, THE TIME

100
bǐ
百

101
ēebǐlíng·ēe
一百零一

200
lyárngbǐ
二百

202
èrbǐlíng·èr
二百零二

1,000
chyēn
千

2,000
lyǎrng·chyēn
二千

10,000
wàn
万

1,000,000
bǐwàn
百万

100,000,000
ēe
亿

see also grammar section

1st
dèe ēe
第一

2nd
dèe èr
第二

3rd
dèe sān
第三

4th
dèe sìr
第四

5th
dèe wǔ
第五

6th
dèe lyò
第六

7th
dèe chēe
第七

8th
dèe bā
第八

9th
dèe jyǒ
第九

10th
dèe shír
第十

what's the date?
jīntyēn jěehào?
今天几号？

it's the first of June
jīntyēn lyò yewèh ēehào
今天六月一号

1994
ēejyójyǒsìr nyén
一九九四年

what time is it?
jéedyěnler?
几点了？

it's midday/midnight
syèndzì jōngwǔ/bànyèh
现在中午/半夜

71

NUMBERS, THE DATE, THE TIME

it's one/three o'clock
syèndzì
ēedyěnler/sāndyěnler

现在一点了 / 三点了

it's twenty past three
syèndzì sāndyěn èrshír

现在三点二十

it's twenty to three
syèndzì chā èrshír
sāndyěn

现在差二十三点

**it's half past eight/half past
nine**
syèndzì
bādyěnbàn/jyódyěnbàn

现在八点半 / 九点半

it's a quarter past five
syèndzì wúdyěn ēekèr

现在五点一刻

it's quarter to five
syèndzì chā ēekèr
wúdyěn

现在差一刻五点

at two/five o'clock
dzì lyárngdyěn/wúdyěn

在二点 / 五点

ENGLISH-CHINESE

A

a
(see grammar)

about *(approx)*
dàgì — 大概

above
dzì . . .
shàrngmyèn — 在……上面

accident
shìrgù — 事故

acrobatics
dzájèe — 杂技

acupuncture
jēnjyǒ — 针灸

adaptor *(for voltage)*
byènyāchèe — 变压器

(plug)
dwōryòng
chātó — 多用插头

address
dèejìr — 地址

adult
dàrén — 大人

aeroplane
fāyjēe — 飞机

after
ēehò — 以后

afternoon
syàwǔ — 下午

afterwards
hòlı — 后来

again
dzì — 再

against: I'm against it
wór fāndwày — 我反对

age
nyénjèe — 年纪

agent
dìlěerén — 代理人

ago
ēechyén — 以前

three days ago
sān tyēn
ēechyén — 三天以前

agree: I agree
wǒr tóng·èe — 我同意

AIDS
ìdzīrbìng — 艾滋病

air
kōngchèe — 空气

air-conditioning
kōngtyáo — 空调

airmail: by airmail
hárngkōngsyìn — 航空信

airport
fāyjēechǎrng — 飞机场

alarm clock
nàojōng — 闹钟

alcohol
jyǒjīng — 酒精

alive
hwórjer — 活着

all
swóryǒ — 所有

73

ENGLISH-CHINESE

allergic to
dwày ... yŏ
gwòrmĭn
fănyìng
对……有
过敏反应

allowed
yéwnsyĕwder
允许的

all right: that's all right
syíng
行

almost
chàbudwŏr
差不多

alone
dāndú
单独

also
yĕh
也

altogether
éegòng
一共

always
dzŏngshìr
总是

ambulance
jyòhùchēr
救护车

America
Mǎygwór
美国

amp: 13-amp
13 ānpáy
13 安培

and
hér
和

angry
shērngchèe
生气

ankle
jyǎobórdzir
脚脖子

another (*different*)
lìng éegèr
另个
(*extra*)
yŏ éegèr
又一个

another beer
yòlì éegèr
péejyŏ
又来一个啤酒

answer
hwáydá
回答

antibiotic
kàrngjĕwnsù
抗菌素

antihistamine
kàrngdzŭan
抗组胺

antiseptic
fárngfŭjèe
防腐剂

apartment
dān-yewén
单元

appendicitis
lánwăy·yén
阑尾炎

apple
pínggwŏr
苹果

appointment
yewéh·hwày
约会

apricot
syìngdzir
杏子

April
sìr·yewèh
四月

arm
gērbor
胳膊

arrest
dìbŭ
逮捕

arrive
dào
到

art
èeshù
艺术

artist
èeshùjyā
艺术家

ashtray
yēnhwāygārng
烟灰缸

ask
wèn
问

asleep
shwàyjáoler
睡着了

aspirin
āsīrpĕelín
阿司匹林

asthma
syàochwăn
哮喘

74

ENGLISH-CHINESE

at
dzì
在

  at the station
dzì chērjàn
在车站

  at Xiao Wang's
dzì Syǎo
Wárng jyā
在小王家

attractive
mírénder
迷人的

August
bā·yewèh
八月

aunt (*maternal*)
éemā
姨妈

  (*paternal*)
gūmā
姑妈

Australia
Àodàlèeyà
澳大利亚

automatic
dzìrdòng
自动

autumn
chyōtyēn
秋天

awake
syǐngjer
醒着

awful
dzāotòler
糟透了

axle
jó
轴

B

baby
yīng·ér
婴儿

back
hwáy
回

  go back
hwáy chèw
回去

  come back
hwáy lí
回来

back (*of body*)
bày
背

bad
hwì
坏

bag
sùlyàodì
(*suitcase*)
syārngdzir
塑料袋
箱子

baggage check
(*US*)
syínglěe
jèetsúnchù
行李寄存处

baker
myènbāofárng
面包房

bald
tūtú
秃头

ball
chyó
球

bamboo
júdzir
竹子

banana
syārngjyāo
香蕉

bandage
bērngdì
绷带

bank
yínhárng
银行

bar
jyǒbā
酒吧

barber
lěefàdyèn
理发店

bath
syéedzǎo
洗澡

bathroom
syéedzǎojyēn
洗澡间

battery
dyènchír
电池

be
shìr; (*see
grammar*)
是

ENGLISH-CHINESE

beach
hǐtān
海滩

beans
dòudzir
豆子

beard
húdzir
胡子

beautiful
mǎylèe
美丽

because
yīnway
因为

bed
chwárng
床

bedroom
wòrshìr
卧室

bee
mèefērng
蜜蜂

beef
nyóròu
牛肉

beer
péejyǒ
啤酒

before
dzǐ . . .
ěechyén
在……以前

begin
kǐshǐr
开始

behind
dzǐ . . . hòmyen
在……后面

bell
jōng
钟
(*for door*)
líng
铃

below
dzǐ . . . syàmyèn
在……下面

belt
yāodì
腰带

bend
jwǎnwān
转弯

best: the best
dzwàyhǎo
最好

better
hǎo ěedyǎrr
好一点

between
dzǐ . . . jīrjyēn
在……之间

bicycle
dzìr·syíngchēr
自行车

big
dà
大

bill
jàrngdān
账单

bird
nyǎo
鸟

biro (*R*)
yewén·jūběe
元珠笔

birthday
shěrngrìr
生日

biscuit
bǐnggān
饼干

bit: a little bit
ěedyǎrr
一点

bite (*insect*)
yǎo
咬

black
hāy
黑

blanket
tǎndzir
毯子

blind
syā
瞎

blocked
dǔjùler
堵住了

blond
jīnhwárngsèr
金黄色

blood
syew·èh
血

blouse
něwchènshān
女衬衫

blue
lánsèr
蓝色

ENGLISH-CHINESE

glasses
yěnjìng
眼镜

gloves
shŏutào
手套

glue
jyāoshwǎy
胶水

go
chèw
去

go away
léekī
离开

go away!
gǔn!
滚！

Gobi Desert
Gērbèetān
戈壁滩

go in
jìnchèw
进去

go out
chūchèw
出去

go down
syàchèw
下去

go up
shàrngchèw
上去

go through
chwān·gwòr
穿过

God
Shàrngdèe
上帝

gold
hwárngjīn
黄金

good
hǎo
好

goodbye
dzàijyèn
再见

got: have you got ...?
née yǒ ... ma?
你有……吗？

government
jèrngfǔ
政府

grammar
yéwfǎ
语法

grandfather
(maternal)
wìgōng
外公

(paternal)
yéyeh
爷爷

grandmother
(maternal)
wìpór
外婆

(paternal)
nǐnǐ
奶奶

grapefruit
yòdzir
柚子

grapes
pútao
葡萄

grass
tsǎo
草

grateful
gǎnjēe
感激

greasy
yónèe
油腻

green
lèwsèr
绿色

grey
hwāysèr
灰色

grocer
dzáhwòrdyèn
杂货店

ground floor
dèe ēe ló
第一楼

group
syáodzǔ
小组

guarantee
bǎosyō
保修

guest
kèr·ren
客人

guide
dǎoyó
导游

guidebook
dǎoyó
shǒtsèr
导游手册

ENGLISH-CHINESE

guitar
jéetā
吉他

gun (*pistol*)
shǒchyǎrng
手枪
(*rifle*)
chyǎrng
枪

hair
tófa
头发

haircut
lěefà
理发

hairdresser
lěefàdyèn
理发店

half
éebàn
一半

half an hour
bàn syǎoshir
半小时

ham
hwórtwǎy
火腿

hamburger
hànbǎobāo
汉堡包

hammer
chwáydzir
锤子

hand
shǒ
手

handbag
shǒtéebāo
手提包

handkerchief
shǒjwèn
手绢

handle (*of door etc*)
báshǒ
把手

hand luggage
shǒtée
syínglěe
手提行李

handsome
yīngjèwn
英俊

happy
kwīlèr
快乐

harbour
gárngkǒ
港口

hard (*material*)
yìng
硬
(*difficult*)
nán
唯

hat
màodzir
帽子

hate
hèn
恨

have
yǒ
有

I have to ...
wór dǎy ...
我得......

hay fever
hwāfěnrèr
花粉热

he
tā; (*see grammar*)
他

head
tó
头

headache
tótérng
头疼

headlights
chērtóděrng
车头灯

health: your health!
jù něe
jyènkārng
祝你健康

hear
tīngjyèn
听见

hearing aid
jùtīngchèe
助听器

heart
syīndzàrng
心脏

heart attack
syīnjēe
gěrngsèr
心肌哽塞

90

ENGLISH-CHINESE

heat
rèr 热

heating
nwǎnchèe 暖气

heavy
jòng 重

heel *(of shoe)*
gērr 跟

(of foot)
jyǎogēn 脚跟

helicopter
jírshērng 直升飞机
fāyjēe

hello
née hǎo 你好

help
bārngjù 帮助

help!
jyòmìng! 救命！

her *(possessive)*
tāder 她的

(object)
tā; *(see 她
grammar)*

herbs *(cooking)*
dzwǒrlyào 佐料

(medicine)
tsǎoyào 草药

here
jèrr 这儿

hers
tāder; *(see 她的
grammar)*

hiccups
dǎgér 打嗝

high
gāo 高

hill
shān 山

him
tā; *(see 他
grammar)*

hip
túnbù 臀部

hire: for hire
chǔdzū 出租

his
tāder; *(see 他的
grammar)*

hit *(verb)*
dǎ 打

hitchhike
dābyènchēr 搭便车

hole
dòng 洞

holiday
jyàchēe 假期

(public)
jyéh·rìr 节日

home
jyā 家

at home
dzì jyā 在家

(in my country)
dzì wǒrmen 在我们国家
gwórjyā

go home
hwáy jyā 回家

honey
fērngmèe 蜂蜜

Hong Kong
Syārnggǎrng 香港

hope *(verb)*
syēewàrng 希望

horrible
kěr pà 可怕

horse
mǎ 马

ENGLISH-CHINESE

hospital
ēe·yewèn 医院

hospitality
rèrchíng hàokèr 热情好客

hot
hěn rèr 很热
(to taste)
là 辣

hotel (superior, for foreigners)
fàndyèn 饭店
(small)
léwgwǎn 旅馆

hour
syǎoshír 小时

house
fárngdzir 房子

how?
dzěmmer 怎么
how are you?
née hǎo ma? 你好吗 ?
how are things?
éechyèh dō hǎo ma? 一切都好吗 ?
how many?
dwōrshao? 多少 ?
how much?
dwōrshao? 多少 ?

hungry: I'm hungry
wǒr èrler 我饿了

hurry up!
kwì dyàrr! 快点 !

hurt: it hurts
térng 疼

husband
jàrngfu 丈夫

I

I
wǒr; (see grammar) 我

ice
bīng 冰

ice cream
bīngchéelín 冰淇淋

idiot
shǎgwā 傻瓜

if
rúgwǒr 如果

ignition
dyénhwǒr 点火

ill
shērngbìngler 生病了

immediately
mǎshàrng 马上

important
jòngyào 重要

impossible
bù kěrnérng 不可能

in
dzì 在

in London
dzì Lúndūn 在伦敦
in English
yòng Yīngyěw 用英语
is he in?
tā dzì ma? 他在吗 ?

included
bāokwòr dzìnày 包括在内

India
Yìndù 印度

92

indigestion
syáohwà bù lyárng　消化不良

industry
gōngyèh　工业

infection
gánrǎn　感染

information
syìnsyēe　信息

injection
jùshèr　注射

injured
shòshārngler　受伤了

inner tube
nàytī　内胎

innocent
wúgū　无辜

insect
kūnchóng　昆虫

insect repellent
chēwchóngjèe　驱虫剂

insurance
báosyěn　保险

intelligent
tsōngming　聪明

interesting
yǒ èesir　有意思

invitation
yāochīng　邀请

Ireland
lĕrlán　爱尔兰

iron (metal)
tyěh　铁
(for clothes)
yèwndǒ　熨斗

ironmonger
wǔjīn shārngdyèn　五金商店

island
dǎo　岛

it
tā　它
it is . . .
tā shìr . . .; (see grammar)　它是……

J

jack (car)
chyēnjīndǐng　千斤顶

jacket
shàrng·ēe　上衣

jade
yèw　玉

jam
gwǒrjyàrng　果酱

January
ēe·yewèh　一月

Japan
Rìben　日本

jasmine tea
mòrlèehwā chá　茉莉花茶

jaw
syà èr　下颚

jazz
jwéshìr yīn·yewèh　爵士音乐

jeans
nyódzǐkù　牛仔裤

jewellery
shǒshìr　首饰

job
gōngdzwòr　工作

joke
syàohwà　笑话

journey
lěwsyíng　旅行

ENGLISH-CHINESE

have a good journey!
éelù shùnfērng!
一路顺风！

jug
gwàndzir
罐子

juice
gwǒrjīr
果汁

July
chēe·yewèh
七月

junction (*road*)
jyāochākǒ
交叉口

June
lyò·yewèh
六月

just: just two
jīryào lyǎrnggèr
只要二个

knee
syēegì
膝盖

knife
dāodzir
刀子

know
jīrdào
知道
(*person*)
rènshìr
认识

I don't know
wǒr bù jīrdào
我不知道

Korea: North Korea
Bǎy Cháosyěn
北朝鲜

South Korea
Nán Cháosyěn
南朝鲜

K

key
yàoshir
钥匙

kidney
shèn
肾
(*to eat*)
yǎodzir
腰子

kill
shā
杀

kilo
gōngjīn
公斤

kilometre
gōnglěe
公里

kind
hén hǎo
很好

kiss
wěn
吻

kitchen
chúfárng
厨房

L

ladder
tēedzir
梯子

ladies (*room*)
něw tsèrswǒr
女厕所

lady
něwshìr
女士

lake
hú
湖

lamb
yárng·rò
羊肉

lamp
dērng
灯

language
yěwyén
语言

Laos
Lǎowǒr
老挝

large
dà
大

last
dzwàyhò
最后

ENGLISH-CHINESE

last year
chèw·nyén
去年

late
wǎn
晚

laugh
dà syào
大笑

laundry (*to wash*)
yào syěe der
ēefu
要洗的衣服
(*place*)
syěe·ēedyèn
洗衣店

law
fǎlèw
法律

lawn
tsǎopíng
草坪

lawyer
lèwshïr
律师

laxative
syèyào
泻药

lazy
lǎn
懒

leaflet
shwōrmíngshū
说明书

leak
lò
漏

learn
syewéh
学

leather
péegér
皮革

leave (*behind*)
dyōsyà
丢下
(*go away*)
léekï
离开
(*forget*)
bǎ . . .
wàrngler
把……忘了

left
dzwǒr
左

on the left (of)
dzì . . .
dzwǒrbyēn
在左边

left·handed
dzwórpyědzir
左撇子

left luggage
sýínglèe
jèetsúnchù
行李寄存处

leg
twǎy
腿

lemon
níngmérng
柠檬

lemonade
níngmérng
chèeshwǎy
柠檬汽水

lemon tea
níngmérngchá
柠檬茶

lens (*camera*)
jǐngtó
镜头

less
shāo ēesyēh
少一些

lesson
kèr
课

letter (*in mail*)
sýìn
信

letterbox
sýìnsyārng
信箱

library
túshūgwǎn
图书馆

licence
jírjiào
执照

lid
gìdzir
盖子

lie down
tǎrngsyà
躺下

life
shērnghwór
生活

lift (*elevator*)
dyèntēe
电梯

95

ENGLISH-CHINESE

light (*in room etc*)
dērng
灯

have you got a light?
jyèh ger hwǒr, syíng ma?
借个火, 行吗?

light (*adjective*)
chīng
轻

light bulb
dērngpào
灯泡

lighter
dáhwǒrjēe
打火机

like: I like ...
wǒr syěehwān ...
我喜欢......

I would like ...
wǒr syǎrng ...
我想......

like (*as*)
syàrng
象

lip
dzwǎychún
嘴唇

lipstick
kǒhóng
口红

listen (to)
tīng
听

litre
shērng
升

little
syǎo
小

a little bit (of)
ēe dyén dyen
一点点

live
jù
住

liver
gān
肝

living room
kèrtīng
客厅

lock
swǒr
锁

long
chárng
长

a long time
hén jyǒ
很久

look: look (at)
kàn
看

look (*seem*)
kànshàrngchèw
看上去

look like
syàrng
象

look for
jāo
找

look out!
syǎosyīn!
小心!

lorry
kǎchēr
卡车

lose
dyōshīr
丢失

lost property office
shīrwù jāolǐng chù
失物招领处

lot: a lot (of)
syēw dwōr
许多

loud
dàshērng der
大声的

love
lchíng
爱情

love (*verb*)
ì
爱

lovely (*person*)
kěr ì
可爱

(*thing*)
hén hǎo
很好

low
dēe
低

luck
yèwnchee
运气

good luck!
jù hǎo yèwn!
祝好运!

96

ENGLISH-CHINESE

luggage
syínglěe — 行李

lunch
wǔfàn — 午饭

lungs
fày — 肺

M

mad
fērngler — 疯了

magazine
dzájìr — 杂志

mail
syìnjyèn — 信件

make
dzwòr — 做

make·up
hwàjwārngpǐn — 化妆品

man
nánder — 男的

manager
jīnglěe — 经理

Mandarin
pǔtōnghwà — 普通话

many
hěn dwōr — 很多

Mao Tse Tung jacket
jōngshānjwārng — 中山装

map
dèetú — 地图

March
sān·yewèh — 三月

market
shìrchǎrng — 市场

married
ěehūnder — 已婚的

martial arts
wǔshù — 武术

mascara
jyémáoyó — 睫毛油

match (*light*)
hwǒrchǐ — 火柴
(*sport*)
běe sì — 比赛

material (*cloth*)
bù — 布

matter: it doesn't matter
máy gwānsee — 没关系

mattress
chwárng dyèn — 床垫

May
wǔ·yewèh — 五月

maybe
kěrnérng — 可能

me
wǒr — 我

me too
wór yěh shìr; — 我也是
(*see grammar*)

meal
fàn — 饭

measles
májěn — 麻疹

meat
rò — 肉

medicine
yào — 药

meeting
hwày — 会

melon
gwā — 瓜

mend
syōlěe — 修理

men's room (*US*)
nán tsèrswǒr — 男厕所

97

ENGLISH-CHINESE

menu
tsǐ pǔ
菜谱

message
kǒsyìn
口信

metal
jīnshǔ
金属

metre
měe
米

middle
jōngjyěn
中间

milk
nyóni
牛奶

mine
wǒrder; (see
grammar)
我的

mineral water
kwàrng·
chwénshwǎy
矿泉水

minute
fēn
分

mirror
jìngdzir
镜子

Miss
syáojyěh
小姐

miss (train etc)
wùchēr
误车

I miss you
wǒr hén
syǎrng nyèn
něe
我很想念你

mistake
tswòrwù
错误

modern
syèndì
现代

Monday
syīngchee·ēe
星期一

money
chyén
钱

Mongolia
Mérnggǔ
蒙古

Inner Mongolia
Nàyměrng
内蒙

Outer Mongolia
Wìměrng
外蒙

month
yewèh
月

moon
yewèh·lyàrng
月亮

more
gèrng dwōr
更多

I've no more . . .
wǒr máy yǒ
. . . ler
我没有……了

**no more rice
thanks**
bú yào fàn ler
不要饭了

morning
dzǎoshàrng
早上

mosquito
wéndzir
蚊子

mosquito net
wénjàrng
蚊帐

most (of)
dà dwōrshù
大多数

mother
māma
妈妈

motorbike
mórtwǒrchēr
摩托车

motorway
gāosù gōnglù
高速公路

mountain
shān
山

mouse
láoshǔ
老鼠

moustache
syǎohúdzir
小胡子

mouth
dzwǎyba
嘴巴

98

ENGLISH-CHINESE

movie
dyènyĭng
电影

movie theater (*US*)
dyènyĭng yewèn
电影院

Mr ...
... syēnsherng
……先生

Mrs ...
... fūren
……夫人

Ms ...
... nĕwshìr
……女士

much
dwŏr
多

muscle
jĕerò
肌肉

museum
bórwùgwăn
博物馆

mushrooms
mórgu
蘑菇

music
yīn·yewèh
音乐

must: I/she must
wŏr/tā yīnggI
我/她应该

my
wŏrder; (*see grammar*)
我的

N

nail (*in wall*)
dīngdzir
钉子

nail clippers
jĭrjyă dăo
指甲刀

nail polish
jĭrjyă yó
指甲油

nail polish remover
chèwdyào jĭrjyăyó der
去掉指甲油的

naked
lwórtĕe
裸体

name
míngdzir
名字

what's your name?
nĕe jyào shemmer míngdzir?
你叫什么名字？

my name is Jim
wŏr jyào Jim
我叫 Jim

napkin
tsānjīn
餐巾

nappy
nyàobù
尿布

narrow
jI
窄

nationality
gwórjée
国籍

natural
dzir·rán
自然

near
lée ... hĕnjìn
离……很近

near here
dzì fùjìn
在附近

the nearest ...
dzwàyjìnder ...
最近的……

nearly
chàbudwŏr
差不多

necessary
bèeyào
必要

neck
bórdzir
脖子

necklace
syàrnglyèn
项链

need: I need ...
wŏr syēwyào ...
我需要……

99

ENGLISH-CHINESE

needle
jēn
针

negative (*film*)
děepyèn
底片

Nepal
Néebór·ěr
尼泊尔

nervous
jǐnjārng
紧张

never
tsónglí bù
从来不

new
syīn
新

news
syīnwén
新闻

newspaper
bàojǐr
报纸

New Year
syīnnyén
新年

happy New Year!
Syīnnyénhǎo
新年好

New Zealand
Syīn Syēelán
新西兰

next
syà éegèr
下一个

next to . . .
dzì . . .
párngbyēn
在……旁边

nice
hén hǎo
很好

night
yèh
夜

nightdress
shwàyēe
睡衣

no
bù
不

I've no . . .
wǒr máy yǒ
. . .
我没有
……

no rice thanks
bú yào fàn
不要饭

nobody
máyyǒ·rén
没有人

noise
dzàoyīn
噪音

noisy
hén chǎo
很吵

non·smoking
fǎy syēeyēn
chēw
非吸烟区

normal
jèrngchárng
正常

north
báy
北

nose
béedzir
鼻子

not
bù; (*see grammar*)
不

notebook
běejèebén
笔记本

nothing
máy yǒ
shemmer
没有什么

November
shír·ēe·yewèh
十一月

now
syèndzì
现在

number
hàomǎ
号码

nurse
hùshir
护士

O

October
shír·yewèh
十月

of
. . . der; (*see
grammar*)
……的

ENGLISH-CHINESE

office
bàn·gōngshìr
办公室

often
jīngcháng
经常

oil
yó
油

OK
hǎo
好

I'm OK
wǒr hí syíng
我还行

old (*person*)
lǎo
老

(*things*)
jyò
旧

how old are you?
nēe dwǒrdàler?
你多大了？

I'm 25 years old
wǒr èrshírwǔ swàyler
我二十五岁了

omelette
chǎojēedàn
炒鸡蛋

on
dzì ... shàrngmyen
在……上面

one
ēe
一

onion
yárngtsōng
洋葱

only
jír yǒ
只有

open (*adjective*)
kīler
开了

open (*verb*)
kī
开

opera
gērjèw
歌剧

Peking opera
jīngjèw
京剧

operation
shǒshù
手术

opposite:
opposite the ...
dzì ... dwàymyèn
在……对面

optician
yěnjìngdyèn
眼镜店

or
hwòrjer
或者

orange (*fruit*)
gwārng gān
广柑

(*colour*)
jéhwàrngsèr
桔黄色

orchestra
gwǎnsyén yewèh·dwày
管弦乐队

other
byéder
别的

our(s)
wǒrmender;
(*see grammar*)
我们的

out: she's out
tā bú dzì
她不在

outside
wìmyen
外面

over (*above*)
dzì ... shàrngmyèn
在……上面

over (*finished*)
wánler
完了

over there
dzì nàrr
在那儿

P

package
bāogwǒr
包裹

packet (*of cigarettes etc*)
bāo
一包

paddy field
dàotyén
稻田

page
yèh
页

pagoda
tǎ
塔

pain
térng
疼

painful
térng
疼

painkiller
chèwtòngpyèn
去痛片

painting
hwà
画

panda
syóngmāo
熊猫

pants (*trousers*)
chárng kù
长裤

panties
sānjyǎokù
三角裤

paper
jǐr
纸

parcel
bāogwǒr
包裹

pardon?
něe shwǒrder shemmer?
你说的什么?

parents
fùmǔ
父母

park (*noun*)
gōng·yewén
公园

park (*car*)
tíng chēr
停车

parking lot (*US*)
tíngchērchǎrng
停车场

part
bùfen
部分

party (*celebration*)
wǎnhwày
晚会

party (*group*)
twántěe
团体

pass (*mountain*)
gwānkǒ
关口

passport
hùjào
护照

path
syǎolù
小路

pavement
rénsyíngdào
人行道

pavilion
tíngdzir
亭子

pay
fùchyén
付钱

peach
táodzir
桃子

peanuts
hwāshērng
花生

pear
lée
梨

peas
wāndò
豌豆

pedal
tàbǎn
踏板

pedestrian crossing
rénsyíng hérngdào
人行横道

pen
gǎrngběe
钢笔

pencil
chyēnběe
铅笔

penicillin
chīngmáysù
青霉素

penknife
chyēnběedāo
铅笔刀

ENGLISH-CHINESE

people
rén
人

pepper (*spice*)
húyjyáo
糊椒
(*red/green*)
shìrdzirjyáo
柿子椒

per cent
bǐfēn jīr ...
百分之……

perfect
hǎojéeler
好极了

perfume
syārngshwǎy
香水

period (*woman's*)
yewèh·jīng
月经

person
rén
人

petrol
chèeyó
汽油

petrol station
jyāyójàn
加油站

phone (*verb*)
dǎ dyènhwà
打电话

phone box
dyènhwàtíng
电话亭

phone number
dyènhwàhàomǎ
电话号码

photograph
jàopyèn
照片

photograph (*verb*)
jàosyàrng
照相

phrase book
dwàyhwà
shǒtsèr
对话手册

pickpocket
páshǒ
扒手

piece
kwì; (*see grammar*)
块

pill
yàowán
药丸

pillow
jěntó
枕头

pin
byéjēn
别针

pineapple
bōrlwór
菠萝

pink
fēnhóng
粉红

pipe
gwǎndzir
管子
(*to smoke*)
yēndǒ
烟斗

pity: it's a pity
jēn kěrsyée
真可惜

plane
fāyjēe
飞机

plant
jírwù
植物

plastic
sùlyào
塑料

plastic bag
sùlyàodì
塑料袋

plate
pándzir
盘子

platform (*station*)
jàntí
站台

play (*theatre*)
hwàjèw
话剧

play (*verb*)
wán
玩

pleasant
yéwkwì
愉快

please
chǐng
请

pleased
gāosyìng
高兴

pliers
chyéndzir
钳子

103

ENGLISH-CHINESE

plug (*electric*)
chātó 插头
(*in sink*)
sīdzir 塞子

plum
lĕedzir 李子

pocket
kŏdì 口袋

poison
dú 毒

police
jĭngchá 警察

policeman
jĭngchá 警察

police station
jĭngchájéw 警察局

polite
yó lĕemào 有礼貌

politics
jèrngjìr 政治

polluted
wūrănler der 污染了的

poor
chyóng 穷

pop music
lyósyíng 流行音乐、
yīn·yewèh

pork
jūrò 猪肉

possible
kĕrnérng 可能

post (*verb*)
jèe 寄

postcard
míngsyìnpyèn 明信片

poster
jāotyĕhwà 招贴画

post office
yójéw 邮局

potato
tŭdò 土豆

pound (*money*)
yīngbàrng 英镑

prawn
dwàysyā 对虾

pregnant
hwéyèwn 怀孕

prescription
chŭfârng 处方

present (*gift*)
lĕewù 礼物

pretty
pyàolyarng 漂亮

price
jyàgér 价格

priest
shénfù 神父

prison
jyēnyèw 监狱

private
sīren 私人

problem
kùnnan 困难

pronounce
fāyīn 发音

pull
lā 拉

pump
bèrng 泵

puncture
tsìrpò 刺破

purple
dzīrsèr 紫色

purse
chyénbāo 钱包

push
twāy 推

104

ENGLISH-CHINESE

put
fàrng
放

pyjamas
shwày·ēe
睡衣

Q

question
wèntee
问题

queue
dwàywū
队伍

quick(ly)
kwì
快

quiet
ānjìng
安静

quite (*fairly*)
běejyào
比较

R

rabbit
tùdzir
兔子

radio
shōyīnjēe
收音机

railway
tyělù
铁路

rain
yěw
雨

it's raining
syàyěw ler
下雨了

raincoat
yěw·ēe
雨衣

rape
chyárngjyèn
强奸

raspberry
mùmáy
木莓

rat
láoshǔ
老鼠

raw
shērng
生

razor
gwā húdāo
刮胡刀

razor blade
gwāhú
dāopyèn
刮胡刀片

read
dú
读

ready
jūnbày hǎo
准备好

rear lights
hò chěrdērng
后车灯

receipt
shōjèw
收据

reception (*hotel*)
jyēdìchù
接待处

record (*music*)
chàrngpyèn
唱片

record player
dyènchàrngjēe
电唱机

red
hóngsèr
红色

red·headed
hóng tófa der
红头发的

religion
dzōngjyào
宗教

remember: I
remember
wǒr jèeder
我记得

rent (*verb*)
dzū
租

repair
syōlěe
修理

repeat
chóngfù
重复

ENGLISH-CHINESE

reservation
yèwdìng
预订

rest (*remaining*)
shèrngsyà der
剩下的

rest (*sleep*)
syōsyee
休息

restaurant
fàndyèn
饭店

restroom (*US*)
tsèrswŏr
厕所

reverse (*gear*)
dàochēr
dărng
倒车档

**reverse charge
call**
dwàyfārng
fùkwăn
对方付款

rheumatism
fērngshīrbìng
风湿病

rib
làygŭ
肋骨

rice (*cooked*)
fàn
饭

(*uncooked*)
mĕe
米

rice bowl
fànwăn
饭碗

rice field
dàotyén
稻田

rich
yōchyén
有钱

right (*side*)
yò
右

on the right (of)
dzì yòbyĕn
在右边

right (*correct*)
dwày
对

ring (*on finger*)
jyèjir
戒指

river
hér
河

road
lù
路

roll (*bread*)
myènbāo
jewĕn
面包卷

roof
fárngdĭng
房顶

room
fárng·jyēn
房间

rope
shérngdzir
绳子

rose
máygwày
玫瑰

route
lùsyèn
路线

rubber
syàrngjyāo
橡胶

(*eraser*)
syàrngpée
橡皮

rubber band
syàrngpéejin
橡皮筋

rubbish (*refuse*)
lājèe
垃圾

rucksack
bàybāo
背包

rude
tsŭlŭ
粗鲁

rug
syăo dèetăn
小地毯

ruins
fàysyēw
废墟

rum
lánmújyŏ
兰姆酒

run
păo
跑

Russia
Érgwór
俄国

106

ENGLISH-CHINESE

S

sad
nán·gwòr
难过

safe
ānchwén
安全

safety pin
byéjēn
别针

salad
sèrlā
色拉

salt
yén
盐

same
éeyàrng
一样

sandals
lyárngsyéh
凉鞋

sandwich
sānmíngjìr
三明治

sanitary towel
wàyshērngjīn
卫生巾

Saturday
syīngcheelyò
星期六

sauce
jīr
汁

sausage
syārngchárng
香肠

say
shwōr
说

scarf (*neck*)
wáyjīn
围巾

school
syewéh·syào
学校

scissors
jyēndāo
剪刀

Scotland
Sūgérlán
苏格兰

screwdriver
lwórsīrdāo
螺丝刀

scroll
hwàjó
画轴

sea
hǐ
海

seaside: at the seaside
dzǐ hǐbyēn
在海边

seat
dzwòrway
座位

seatbelt
ānchwéndì
安全带

second (*in time*)
myǎo
秒

see
kànjyen
看见

sell
mì
卖

sellotape (R)
tòmíng jyāodǐ
透明胶带

send
sòng
送
(*letter*)
jèe
寄

separate
fēnkī
分开

September
jyǒ·yewèh
九月

serviette
tsānjīn
餐巾

several
jěeger
几个

sew
férng
缝

sexy
syìnggǎn
性感

shade: in the shade
dzì yīnlyárng chù
在荫凉处

shampoo
syěefàjīng
洗发精

share (*verb*)
fēnsyǎrng
分享

shaving brush
syōmyènshwā
修面刷

shaving foam
gwā hú pàomòr
刮胡泡沫

she
tā; (*see grammar*)
她

sheet
chwárngdān
床单

ship
chwán
船

shirt
chènshān
衬衫

shoe laces
syédì
鞋带

shoe polish
syéyó
鞋油

shoe repairer
syōsyédyèn
修鞋店

shoes
syéh
鞋

shop
shǎrngdyèn
商店

go shopping
chèw mǐ dōngsēe
去买东西

short (*person*) l
矮

(*time*)
dwǎn
短

shorts
dwǎnkù
短裤

shoulder
jyēnbǎrng
肩膀

shower (*wash*)
línyèw
淋浴

shy
hìsyō
害羞

Siberia
Syēebórlèeyà
西伯利亚

sidewalk
rénsyíngdào
人行道

signature
chyēnmíng
签名

silk
sīrchó
丝绸

Silk Road
sīrchó jīr lù
丝绸之路

silver
yín
银

silver foil
yín bór
银箔

similar
syārngsìr
相似

simple (*easy*)
jyěndān
简单

since (*time*)
dzìr tsóng . . .
自从……

sing
chàrnggēr
唱歌

Singapore
Syīnjyāpōr
新加坡

single (*unmarried*)
wàyhún
未婚

sister
jyěmày
姐妹

sit down
dzwòrsyà
坐下

ENGLISH-CHINESE

size
chǐrtsùn
尺寸

skin
péefū
皮肤

skinny
tì shò
太瘦

skirt
chéwndzir
裙子

sky
tyēn kōng
天空

sleep
shwàyjyào
睡觉

sleeper
wòrpù
卧铺

sleeping bag
shwàydì
睡袋

sleeping pill
ānmyényào
安眠药

**sleepy: I'm
sleepy**
wǒr kùnler
我困了

slide (phot)
hwàndērngpyèn
幻灯片

slim
myáotyao
苗条

slippers
twǒrsyéh
拖鞋

slow(ly)
màn
慢

small
syǎo
小

smell (verb)
wén
闻

smile
syào
笑

smoke (noun)
yēn
烟

smoke (verb)
syēeyēn
吸烟

snake
shér
蛇

snow
syewěh
雪

so (big, slow etc)
jèrmer
这么

soap
fáydzào
肥皂

socket
chādzwòr
插座

socks
wàdzir
袜子

soft
rwǎn
软

soft drink
rwán yīnlyào
软饮料

sole (of shoe)
syéděe
鞋底

some
eesyēh
一些

somebody
yǒrén
有人

something
yǒsyēh
dōngsyēe
有些东西

sometimes
yǒ shír
有时

son
érdzir
儿子

song
gēr
歌

soon
bù jyǒ
不久

**sore: I've got a
sore throat**
wǒr hólong
térng
我喉咙疼

sorry
dwàybuchèe
对不起

ENGLISH-CHINESE

I'm sorry dwàybuchěe	对不起	**stamp** yópyào	邮票
so-so mǎmahūhu	马马虎虎	**star** syīngsying	星星
soup tārng	汤	**station** hwǒrchērjàn	火车站
sour swān	酸	**stay** (in hotel etc) jù	住
south nán	南	**steak** nyópí	牛排
soy sauce jyàrng·yó	酱油	**steal** tō	偷
spanner hwór bānshǒ	活扳手	**steamed roll** hwājwǎrr	花卷
spare parts língjyèn	零件	**steep** hén dǒ	很陡
spark plug hwǒrhwǎ sī	火花塞	**steering wheel** fārngsyàrng·pán	方向盘
speak jyǎrng	讲	**still** (adverb) rérngrán	仍然
do you speak ...? née jyǎrng ... ma?	你讲…… 吗？	**stockings** chárngtǒngwà	长统袜
speed limit sùdù syènjìr	速度限制	**stomach** wày	胃
spider jīrjú	蜘蛛	**stomach ache** wàytérng	胃疼
spoke fútyáo	辐条	**stone** shírto	石头
spoon syǎosháorr	小勺	**stop** chērjàn	车站
sport yèwndòng	运动	**stop** (verb) tíngjǐr	停止
spring (season) chūntyēn	春天	**stop!** tíngsyà!	停下！
square (in town) gwárngchǎrng	广场	**store** shārngdyèn	商店
stairs lótēe	楼梯	**storm** bàofěrng·yěw	暴风雨

ENGLISH-CHINESE

story
gùshìr
故事

straight ahead
èejír cháochyén
一直朝前

strange (*odd*)
chéegwì
奇怪

strawberry
tsǎomáy
草莓

stream
syáosyēe
小溪

street
jyēh
街

string
syèeshérng
细绳

stroke (*attack*)
jòng fērng
中风

strong
jwàrng
壮

(*drink*)
lyèh
烈

(*material*)
jyēshir
结实

student
syewéh·shērng
学生

stupid
bèn
笨

suburbs
jyāochēw
郊区

suddenly
tūrán
突然

sugar
tárng
糖

suit
syēejwārng
西装

suitcase
shǒtéesyārng
手提箱

summer
syàtyēn
夏天

sun
tìyárng
太阳

sunburn
shì hāy
晒黑、

Sunday
syīngcheetyēn
星期天

sunglasses
tìyárngjìng
太阳镜

sunstroke
jòngshǔ
中暑

suntan lotion
fárngshìjèe
防晒剂

supermarket
chāojée
shìrchǎrng
超级市场

surname
syìng
姓

sweater
máo·ēe
毛衣

sweet
tárng
糖

(*to taste*)
tyén
甜

swim
yóyǒng
游泳

swimming costume
yóyǒng·ēe
游泳衣

swimming pool
yóyǒngchír
游泳池

swimming trunks
yóyǒngkù
游泳裤

switch (*electric*)
kīgwān
开关

T

table
jwǒrdzir
桌子

111

ENGLISH-CHINESE

table tennis
pīngpārngchyó 乒乓球

Taiwan
Tíwān 台湾

take
ná 拿

take away
(remove) 拿走
nádzǒ

talk
shwōrhwà 说话

tall
gāo 高

Taoism
Dàojyā 道家

tap
shwǎylóngtó 水龙头

tape *(cassette)*
tsírdì 磁带

taste
wàyr 味

taxi
chūdzūchēr 出租车

tea
chá 茶

teach
jyào 教

teacher
lǎoshīr 老师

team
dwày 队

teapot
cháhú 茶壶

telegram
dyènbào 电报

telephone
dyènhwà 电话

television
dyènshìr 电视

temple
myào 庙

tennis
wǎrngchyó 网球

tent
jàrngpérng 帐篷

Terra Cotta Army
Bīngmáyǒng 兵马佣

terrible
jēn dzāogāo 真糟糕

terrific
bàrngjéeler 棒极了

Thailand
Tìgwór 泰国

than
běe ... gèrng 比……更
uglier than ...
běe ... gèrng 比……更
nánkàn 难看

thank
syèh·syeh 谢谢

thank you
syèh·syeh 谢谢

that
nàger 那个

that one
nàger 那个

the
jèr, nà; *(see 这, 那
grammar)*

theatre
jèw·yewèn 剧院

their(s)
tāmender; *(see 他们的
grammar)*

them
tāmen; *(see 他们
grammar)*

112

ENGLISH-CHINESE

then
nà shír
(*after that*)
ránhò
那时
然后

there
nàrr
那儿

there is/are
yǒ . . .
有......

is/are there . . .?
yǒ . . . ma?
有......吗？

**there isn't/aren't
. . .**
máy yǒ . . .
没有......

thermometer
wēndùjèe
温度计

thermos flask
rèrshwǎpíng
热水瓶

these
jèrsyēh
这些

they
tāmen; (*see
grammar*)
他们

thick
hò
厚

thief
syǎo tō
小偷

thigh
dàtwǎy
大腿

thin (*thing*)
báo
薄

(*person*)
shò
瘦

thing
dōngsyee
东西

think
syǎrng
想

**thirsty: I'm
thirsty**
wǒr kókěr
我口渴

this (*adjective*)
jèr
这

this one
jèrger
这个

those
nàsyēh
那些

thread
syèn
线

throat
hólóng
喉咙

through
jīnggwòr
经过

throw
rērng
扔

throw away
rērngdyào
扔掉

thunderstorm
láyyēw
雷雨

Thursday
syīngcheesìr
星期四

Tibet
Syēedzàrng
西藏

ticket
pyào
票

tie (*necktie*)
lǐngdì
领带

tight
jǐn
紧

tights
lyénkùwà
连裤袜

time
shírjyěn
时间

on time
jūnshír
准时

what time is it?
jéedyěn ler?
几点了？

timetable
shírjyěnbyǎo
时间表

tin opener
gwàntó
chěedzir
罐头起子

113

ENGLISH-CHINESE

tip (*money*)
syǎofày
小费

tire (*US*)
lúntī
轮胎

tired
lày
累

tissues
kójǐr
口纸

to
dào
到

I'm going to Beijing/the station
wǒr yào dào Běyjing/chērjàn chěw
我要到北京/车站去

tobacco
yēnsīr
烟丝

today
jīntyēn
今天

toe
jyáojǐr
脚趾

together
ēechěe
一起

toilet
tsèrswǒr
厕所

toilet paper
shójǐr
手纸

tomato
syēēhóngshìr
西红柿

tomorrow
míngtyēn
明天

tongue
shérto
舌头

tonight
jīntyen wǎnsharng
今天晚上

tonsillitis
byěntáosyèn·yén
扁桃腺炎

too (*also*)
yěh
也

too big
tì dà
太大

not too much
bú tì dwōr
不太多

too much
tì dwōr
太多

tooth
yá
牙

toothache
yátérng
牙疼

toothbrush
yáshwā
牙刷

toothpaste
yágāo
牙膏

torch
shǒdyèntōng
手电筒

tourist
yókèr
游客

towel
máojīn
毛巾

town
chérngshìr
城市

track (*US: station*)
jàntí
站台

traditional
chwántǒng
传统

traffic
jyāotōng
交通

traffic jam
jyāotōng dùsī
交通堵塞

traffic lights
hónglèw dērng
红绿灯

train
hwǒrchēr
火车

translate
fānèe
翻译

114

ENGLISH-CHINESE

travel agent
lěwsyíngshèr
旅行社

traveller's cheque
lěwsyíng jìrpyào
旅行支票

tree
shù
树

tremendous
hǎojéeler
好极了

trip
lěwyó
旅游

trousers
chárng kù
长裤

true
jēnder
真的

trunk (*US: car*)
syíngleesyāng
行李箱

try
shìr shir
试试

T-shirt
T syèw·shān
T恤衫

Tuesday
syīngchee·èr
星期二

tunnel
swàydào
隧道

tweezers
nyèdzir
镊子

tyre
lúntī
轮胎

uncle
shūshu
叔叔

under
dzì ... syàmyèn
在……下面

underpants
kùchǎ
裤衩

understand
míngbí
明白

United States
Mǎygwór
美国

university
dàsyewéh
大学

unpleasant
bù dzěmmer·yàrng
不怎么样

until
jírdào
直到

up: up there
dzì nàr
在那儿

upstairs
dzì lóshàrng
在楼上

urgent
jǐnjée
紧急

us
wǒmen; (*see grammar*)
我们

use
yòng
用

useful
yǒyòng
有用

usually
tōngchárng
通常

U

ugly
nánkàn
唯看

umbrella
yéwsǎn
雨伞

V

vaccination
jòng·nyódò
种牛痘

valid
yǒsyào
有效

valley
shāngǔ
山谷

van
syǎo
yèwnhwòrchēr
小运货车

vanilla
syārngtsǎo
香草

vase
hwāpíng
花瓶

VD
syìngbìng
性病

veal
syǎonyórò
小牛肉

vegetables
shūtsì
蔬菜

vegetarian
chīrsù der
吃素的

very
fāychárng
非常
very much
fāychárng
非常

video
lùsyàrng·jēe
录相机

Vietnam
Yewèh·nán
越南

village
tsündzir
村子

vinegar
tsù
醋

visa
chyēnjèrng
签证

visit (place)
tsān·gwān
参观
(people)
bìfǎrng
拜访

voice
shērng·yīn
声音

W

waist
yāo
腰

wait
děrng
等

waiter
jāodì
招待

waitress
jāodì
招待

wake up (oneself)
syǐngler
醒了

Wales
Wāyěrshìr
威尔士

walk (verb)
dzǒulù
走路

walkman (R)
syòjēn
fǎrngyīnjēe
袖珍放音机

wall
chyárng
墙
the Great Wall of China
Chárngchérng
长城

wallet
chyénbāo
钱包

want
yào
要
I want ...
wǒr yào ...
我要……
do you want ...?
něe yào ... ma?
你要……吗？

war
jànjērng
战争

warm
nwǎnhwór
暖和

ENGLISH-CHINESE

wash
syëe
洗

washbasin
syéelyěnchír
洗脸池

washing powder
syëe·ëefěn
洗衣粉

wasp
hwárngfěrng
黄蜂

watch (for time)
shóbyǎo
手表

watch (verb)
kàn
看

water
shwǎy
水

way: this way
(like this)
jèr·yàrng
这样

can you tell me
the way to the
...?
něe nérng
gàosù wǒr
chèw ... der lù
ma?
你能告诉我
去……的路
吗?

we
wǒrmen; (see
grammar)
我们

weak
rwòr
(tea)
dàn
弱
淡

weather
tyēnchèe
天气

wedding
hūnlěe
婚礼

Wednesday
syīngcheesān
星期三

week
syīngchēe
星期

weekend
jōmòr
周末

weight
jònglyàrng
重量

welcome!
hwānyíng!
欢迎！

welcome: you're
welcome
bú kèrchee
不客气

well: he's
well/not well
tā shēnti hén
hǎo/bù hǎo
他身体很好
/不好

well (adverb)
hén hǎo
很好

west
syēe
西

Western-style
syēeshìr
西式

wet
shīr
湿

what?
shémmer?
什么？

what's this?
jèr shìr
shemmer?
这是什么？

what is ...?
... shìr
shemmer?
……是什么？

wheel
lúndzir
轮子

when?
shémmer
shírhò?
什么时候？

where?
nǎrr?
哪儿？

which
nǎ·éegèr
哪一个

white
bísèr
白色

ENGLISH-CHINESE

who?
sháy? 谁？

whose: whose is this?
jèr shir sháyder? 这是谁的？

why?
wàyshemmer? 为什么？

wide
kwān 宽

wife
chēedzir 妻子

win
yíng 赢

wind
fērng 风

window
chwārnghu 窗户

windscreen
dărngfērng bōrlee 挡风玻璃

wine
pútaojyŏ 葡萄酒

winter
dōngtyēn 冬天

wire
tyěsīr 铁丝

with
hér ...
ēechēe 和……一起

without
máyyŏ 没有

without ice
bú yào bīng 不要冰

woman
fùněw 妇女

wonderful
tì hǎoler 太好了

wood
mùtou 木头

wool
yárngmáo 羊毛

word
tsír 词

work
gōngdzwòr 工作

work (*verb*)
gōngdzwòr 工作

it's not working
hwĭler 坏了

world
shìrjyèh 世界

worse
gèrng dzāo 更糟

wrench
bānshŏ 扳手

wrist
shŏwàn 手腕

write
syĕh 写

wrong
tswòr 错

Y

Yangtze Gorges
Chárngjyărng sānsyá 长江三峡

Yangtze River
Chárngjyărng 长江

year
nyén 年

yellow
hwárngsèr 黄色

Yellow River
Hwárnghér 黄河

Yellow Sea
Hwárnghĭ 黄海

ENGLISH-CHINESE

yes
shìrder; (*see grammar*)　是的

yesterday
dzwórtyēn　昨天

yet: not yet
hí máyner　还没呢

yoghurt
swānnǐ　酸奶

you
nèe　你
(*plural*)
nèemen; (*see grammar*)　你们

young
nyénchīng　年轻

young people
nyénchīngrén　年轻人

your(s)
nèeder　你的
(*plural*)
nèemender; (*see grammar*)　你们的

zero
líng　零

zip
lālyèn　拉链

zoo
dòngwù·yewén　动物园

STRUCTURE

In the south-east of China, Pidgin English was used for
three hundred years by foreigners trading with the
Chinese. In some ways, colloquial Chinese and Pidgin
English are like each other, in their simple structure,
small vocabulary, and wide use of a few basic verbs:

> wŏr chèw kàn kàn
> (*I go look look*)
> **I'll go and have a look**

A Chinese sentence is like a string of beads or a row of
pebbles, chosen and arranged for conciseness and
clarity. Nothing declines or conjugates. Word order is
similar to English, subject — verb — object:

> wŏr yào jày ger
> **I want this one**

There are no *ARTICLES*, no words for **a** and **the** in
Chinese, so for example:

> yínháng
> **the bank, a bank, the banks, banks**

> fùjìn yŏ yínháng ma?
> (*neighbourhood there is bank 'question word'?*)
> **is there a bank near here?**

SINGULAR and *PLURAL* forms are not distinguished,
so for example:

> rén
> **man, men**

If need be, the words for **one** or **some, many** etc, are
added:

> ēe gèr rén   hĕn dwŏr rén
> **one man, a man**   **a lot of men**

GRAMMAR

An *ADJECTIVE* is often introduced by the word 'hěn' **very**:

    hén hǎo
    (very good)
    excellent

    hén hǎo chīr
    (very good eat)
    delicious

    hěn pyàolyàrng
    (very pretty)
    lovely

The verb *TO BE* is normally omitted in basic sentences like:

    tā hén hǎo
    (he very good)
    he's an excellent person

    tsì hén hǎo chīr
    (food very good eat)
    the food is delicious

    fērngjíng hěn pyàolyàrng
    (scenery very pretty)
    the scenery is splendid

When the word order is changed, with the adjective coming before the noun, the word 'der' is added:

    hén hǎo chīr der tsì
    (very good eat 'der' vegetables)
    delicious vegetables

    hěn pyàolyàrng der fērngjǐng
    (very pretty 'der' scenery)
    splendid scenery

The word 'der' can be added to a verb in the following way:

    dzǒder hěn màn
    (go 'der' very slow)
    we're going very slowly!

    gwòrder hěn kwìlèr
    (pass 'der' very happy)
    we're having a very happy time

GRAMMAR

The *COMPARATIVE* is often understood from the context:

nă-ēeger hăo?   jèrger hăo
(which one good)   *(this one good)*
which is better?   **this is better**

Than is 'bĕe':

jèrger bĕe nàyger hăo
(this than that good)
this is better than that

For *SUPERLATIVES* the word 'dzwày' **most** is used:

syăo Wárng dzwày pàrng
(little Wang most fat)
little Wang is the fattest

PERSONAL PRONOUNS are:

wŏr	**I/me**	wŏrmen	**we/us**
nĕe	**you**	nĕemen *(pl)*	**you**
tā	**he/him, she/her**	tāmen	**they/them**

There is a respect form of **you**, 'nín', used in speaking to old or senior people:

nín chīng zwòr
(you please sit)
please have a seat

Pronouns are often left out in Chinese:

jăo sháy?   jăo pérngyŏ
(seek who?)   *(seek friends)*
who are you looking for?   **I'm looking for my
                               friends**

jīntyĕn hăo rèr
(today good hot)
it's very hot today

Pronouns are used for emphasis:

wŏr bú hwày Hànyĕw kĕrshìr tā hwày
(I not can Chinese but he can)
I don't speak Chinese but he does

122

GRAMMAR

POSSESSIVE ADJECTIVES and *POSSESSIVE PRONOUNS* are formed by adding 'der' to the pronoun:

wŏrder	**my/mine**
nĕeder	**your/yours**
tāder	**his, her/hers, its**
wŏrmender	**our/ours**
nĕemender	**your/yours** (*pl*)
tāmender	**their/theirs**
tāder jyā	nà shìr wŏrmender
his home	**that's ours**

VERBS do not change at all — there is only one form. If need be, other words are added to make the sense clear. For example:

> lí

can mean all of:

> **come, comes, came, will come, come!**
>
> tā lí
> **he/she comes, he/she came, he/she will come**
>
> tā dzwórtyēn lí
> **he/she came yesterday**

Normally the context will make the time reference of a verb clear. Words like **tomorrow** or **yesterday** remove any ambiguity.

EXPRESSING THE PRESENT

tā hĕn lày	nĕe zwòr shemmer?
(*he very tired*)	(*you do what*)
he's very tired	**what are you doing?**

wŏr bù syĕehwān yīn-yewèh
(*I not like music*)
I don't like music

EXPRESSING THE FUTURE

míngtyēn dzŏ	wŏr bú chèw
(*tomorrow go*)	(*I not go*)
we're off tomorrow	**I'm not going**

GRAMMAR

EXPRESSING THE PAST (see also *PARTICLES*)

tā zwórtyēn lí
(he yesterday come)
he came yesterday

máy yŏ chèw
(not have go)
I didn't go

YES/NO

Although there are words that can be used for **yes/no**, the usual way to say **yes** or **no** is by repeating a word in the question:

něe hwày yóyŏng ma?
(you can swim 'question word'?)
can you swim?

hwày!
(can)
yes

For **no** you add 'bù':

něe lí ma?
(you come 'question word'?)
are you coming?

bù lí
(not come)
no

QUESTIONS are formed by adding 'ma':

něe yào chèw
(you want go)
you want to go

něe yào chèw ma?
(you want go 'question word'?)
do you want to go?

Another way of asking questions is the form:

lày bú lày?
(tired not tired?)
are you tired?

márng bù márng?
(busy not busy)
are you busy?

GRAMMAR

Special question words:

who?	sháy?	
	sháy yào chèw?	**who wants to go?**
	(who want go?)	
what?	shemmer?	
	shwōr shemmer?	**what are you**
	(say what?)	**saying?**
when?	shemmer shírhò?	
	shemmer shírhò yŏ kòng?	**when are you free?**
	(what time have free?)	
what time?	jée dyĕn?	
	jée dyén dzŏ?	**what time are we going?**
	(what time go?)	
where?	nărr?	
	tā dzì nărr?	**where is he?**
	(he at where?)	
	tā dào nărr?	**where has he gone to?**
	(he to where?)	
why?	wày shemmer?	
	wày shemmer bú chèw?	**why aren't you going?**
	(why not go?)	
how long?	dwōrshăo shírjyēn?	
	yào dwōrshăo shírjyēn?	**how long does it take?**
	(want how much time?)	
how much?	dwōrshăo?	
	jèr dwōrshăo chyén?	**how much is this?**
	(this how much money?)	
how many?	jĕeger?	
	née yó jĕeger syăohí?	**how many children do you have?**
	(you have how many children?)	

To form *NEGATIVES* the main word for **not** is 'bù':

> tā bù lí
> *(he not come)*
> **he's not coming**

GRAMMAR

But before 'yŏ' **have**, **not** is 'máy':

née yŏ máy yŏ chyén?	máy yŏ
(you have not have money?)	*(not have)*
do you have money?	**no, I don't (have any)**

When referring to the past **not** is 'máy':

tā máy lí
(he not come)
he didn't come

NUMBERS do not immediately precede nouns, as they do in English. A *COUNT WORD* must be inserted. This resembles the English **a slice of bread, a bar of chocolate, a packet of crisps.** Often, the count word is 'gèr':

sān gèr rén	ée gèr pínggwŏr
3 people	**1 apple**

But sometimes 'gèr' will not do. Long, thin objects may have the count word 'tyáo':

ée tyáo hér	ée tyáo shér
a river	**a snake**

Flat, thin objects may use 'jārng':

ée jārng jìr	lyărng jārng jwŏrdzir
a piece of paper	**two tables**

Other useful count words are:

wày:	ée wày syēnshērng	sìr wày tìtì
	a gentleman	**four ladies**
kwì:	ée kwì ...	
	a portion/piece (of bread, soap etc)	
wăn:	ée wăn	
	a bowl (of rice/soup etc)	

Two is only 'èr' when counting:

ée èr sān sìr
one two three four

Otherwise, it is 'lyărng':

lyărng gèr pérngyŏ
2 friends

GRAMMAR

Chinese uses *PARTICLES* to modify the meaning of a verb.

'ler' **finish** is added for a process that has reached completion:

> chĕr lí ler
> *(bus come finish)*
> **the bus is here**

> shwăy kī ler
> *(water boil finish)*
> **the water's boiling**

> dào ler
> *(arrive finish)*
> **here we are!**

'hăo' **good, ready** is added for a job that is done:

> jŭnbày hăo
> *(prepare ready)*
> **it's ready**

> bàn hăo
> *(negotiate ready)*
> **it's arranged**

> syōlée hăo
> *(repair ready)*
> **it's fixed**

'ba' is added for a suggestion:

> dzŏ ba!
> **let's be off!**

'ner' means **what about?**:

> wŏr chèw, nĕe ner?
> **I'm going, what about you?**

'gwòr' **pass** is used for things one has done:

> nĕe chèwgwòr Măygwór ma?
> *(you go 'pass' America 'question word'?)*
> **have you been to America?**

OF is translated using 'der' (which is equivalent to **'s**):

> lăo Wárng der jyā
> **Lao Wang's home**

> tāder jyā
> **his house**

> léwgwăn der míngdzir
> **the name of the hotel**

CONVERSION TABLES

metres
  1 metre = 39.37 inches or 1.09 yards

kilometres
  1 kilometre = 0.62 or approximately⅝ mile

to convert kilometres to miles: divide by 8 and multiply by 5

kilometres:	2	3	4	5	10	100
miles:	1.25	1.9	2.5	3.1	6.25	62.5

miles
to convert miles to kilometres: divide by 5 and multiply by 8

miles:	1	3	5	10	20	100
kilometres:	1.6	4.8	8	16	32	160

kilos
  1 kilo = 2.2 or approximately 1⅕ pounds

to convert kilos to pounds: divide by 5 and multiply by 11

kilos:	4	5	10	20	30	40
pounds:	8.8	11	22	44	66	88

pounds
  1 pound = 0.45 or approximately ⁵⁄₁₁ kilo

litres
  1 litre = approximately 1¾ pints or 0.22 gallons

Celsius
to convert to Fahrenheit: divide by 5, multiply by 9, add 32

Celsius:	10	15	20	25	28	30	34
Fahrenheit:	50	59	68	77	82	86	93

Fahrenheit
to convert Fahrenheit to Celsius: subtract 32, multiply by 5,
divide by 9